CELTICS READY FOR TIPOFF

>Steve Bulpett, *Boston Herald*

November 1, 2007

Let us start with one immutable fact: The New Three is not the Big Three.

Kevin Garnett, Paul Pierce and Ray Allen are not Larry Bird, Robert Parish and Kevin McHale. This is not to say they are better or worse, just different. Comparisons seem unfair, in that they are of different individual skill sets and, of major import, the latest triumvirate has not yet had a real opportunity to grow and play together.

But the 2007-08 version of Three Stars on Parquet does have the advantage of being able to learn from history. Making things work on any team in any sport is a chemistry experiment with highly explosive ingredients. Such an experiment can be even more dangerous when the power of the elements is increased.

So why were the Celtics of the 1980s able to channel the greatness of three Hall of Famers? The key may have been the individual character of Bird, Parish and McHale. While insecurity abounds all over the sporting landscape, it may be hard to find three people more comfortable in their own skin.

This was significant both on and off the court, as each realized his place in the machine and was content to defer to the greater good. Bird needed to be cocky to be good, and the others knew he would back it up. Though Parish could have scored more in a different setting, he sat back a bit and understood that the looks he did get would be better because Bird's defender would not be so quick to help out. McHale saw things essentially the same, though it can be argued he was at least as beneficial to Bird as vice versa.

Remember, when the Celts played Atlanta, McHale, not Bird, had to chase Dominique Wilkins. And Parish moved over to deal with Kevin Willis, leaving Larry to guard the in-offensive Tree Rollins.

But McHale went beyond the floor to keep the natural order of things intact in the late '80s. At one point when his contract was up and he could have cashed in big, McHale, according to then-GM Jan Volk, told the club he knew his new deal had to be for less per year than Bird. The sides settled on a contract in less than a day.

It's hard to imagine something similar happening these days, and the guy in Bird's position probably wouldn't want it, knowing that a better deal by a teammate would just increase his own price when it was his turn. That point has largely been made moot by the collective bargaining agreement and its maximum contract levels, but you get the idea.

Parish and McHale were secure enough in their own abilities to know and accept that Bird would be "The Show," something Larry explained to the late radio play-by-play man Johnny Most in one of the funnier moments of the era.

Garnett may be the brightest new star in the Green galaxy, but he's taken giant steps to include Pierce and Allen in his activities. It's not a stretch. The three have hung out together and clearly enjoy each other's company. But they should not be concerned if they find themselves going separate ways as the season wears on.

Bird, Parish and McHale were not regular dinner companions. As one Celtic from the time put it, "They were just different people socially."

They listened to different music and had their own sets of friends. Bird and McHale would even tweak each other at times.

But they all had a trust that when push came to postseason, they could count on each other. And that is where reputations, and cool nicknames, are made.

You can call Kevin Garnett, Paul Pierce and Ray Allen what you want, but before they can approach the legacy of the Big Three, they will have to be called something else.

World Champions.

Sweet 17

Boston Celtics 2007-08 NBA Champions

President and Publisher: Patrick J. Purcell
Editor-in-Chief: Kevin R. Convey
Executive Sports Editor: Hank Hryniewicz
Deputy Sports Editor: Mark Murphy
Director of Photography: Jim Mahoney
Chief Librarian: Al Thibeault
Vice President/Promotion: Gwen Gage

SportsPublishingLLC.com

PUBLISHER: Jim Pouba
PRESIDENT: Mike Callaghan
CHIEF OPERATING OFFICER: Leonard Halpin
VICE PRESIDENT OF SALES: Don Kapral
SENIOR MANAGING EDITOR: Susan M. Moyer
ACQUISITIONS EDITOR: Noah Adams Amstadter
VICE PRESIDENT OF ACQUISITIONS: Doug Hoepker
EDITOR: Amber Greviskes
BOOK LAYOUT: Carl Bezuidenhout

Front cover photo by Matt Stone/Boston Herald
Back cover photo by Matt Stone/Boston Herald

ISBN: 978-1-59670-312-4

This book is available in quantity at special discounts for your group or organization.
For further information, contact the publisher.

Printed in the United States

Sports Publishing L.L.C.
804 North Neil Street
Champaign, IL 61820

Phone: 1-877-424-2665
Fax: 217-363-2073
Web site: www.SportsPublishingLLC.com

MATT STONE/BOSTON HERALD

Above: Kevin Garnett poses with new team-mates Paul Pierce and Ray Allen. JOHN WILCOX, BOSTON HERALD

Left: Kevin Garnett huddles with team-mates during the team's trip to Rome for the NBA Europe Live Tour. NANCY LANE, BOSTON HERALD

Team captain Paul Pierce led the charge on opening night for Boston, scoring a game-high 28 points.
STUART CAHILL, BOSTON HERALD

IT LOOKS PRETTY EASY BEING GREEN

>Mark Murphy, *Boston Herald*
November 3, 2007

Paul Pierce said earlier this week he was no longer star-struck.

No wonder why Shaquille O'Neal once nicknamed him "The Truth."

The Celtics captain, with his new revue making its debut last night, knew of what he spoke:

It's time for the rest of the league to be star-struck by what a lineup featuring Pierce, Kevin Garnett and Ray Allen can do.

Let's just say the goods came as advertised in last night's 103-83 season-opening win over Washington, with the loudest crowd in years laying down a wild soundtrack at TD Banknorth Garden.

"Tonight was rockin', man," said the emotional Garnett, still shaking from the evening's vibe. "I couldn't even help it. This place was rockin'. This place is crazy — (expletive) jacked as you can tell by my first shot, all backboard."

Garnett, a human double-double even when he's at half-speed, debuted with 22 points, 20 rebounds and a devastating fourth-quarter block of Gilbert Arenas that brought the house down in a roaring glee.

Garnett became the first Celtic to notch a 20-20 game since Mark Blount in 2003-04.

The difference: Blount probably will never escape low single figures in that category. Garnett, on the other hand, slapped together the 31st 20-20 game of his career.

Toss in three blocks, three steals and five assists, and you have an idea of how Garnett completely influenced every part of this game. Ray Allen chipped in 17 points on 5-of-10 shooting from the field, and Pierce feasted off the flow with 28 points on 10-of-19 shooting.

The Wizards, on the other hand, missed all 16 of their 3-point attempts, an NBA record for most tries without making one.

Pardon Doc Rivers for stepping in with the mandatory Belichickian attempt at keeping everyone grounded.

"There are many things — I mean many things — that you could tell from this game that we have to work on," said the Celtics coach, whose cautionary words never had a chance against the evidence last night. Best of all for the cyber generation, "Agent Zero," aka Arenas, had to eat his NBA.com blog — the one earlier this week that guaranteed victory. As the crowd showered Arenas with the Yankees treatment, chanting "Gilbert Sucks" every time the Wizards scoring ace touched the ball, Washington sank fast.

It trailed by 18 (48-30) with 3:49 left in the second quarter and by 22 (58-36) at halftime.

By the second half, Arenas was the least of the Wizards in the chippy department. Center Brendan Haywood, talking trash from the start — with some particularly boastful words for Kendrick Perkins after blocking the Celtic center's shot — was finally put in his place.

Garnett, after getting tangled up with Haywood going for a rebound, stepped in the way with some instructive words after the big man shoved Pierce down the other end in the third quarter.

Haywood's line of chatter continued, and his words had the toughness of cheap tissue paper.

Washington had a brief revival with a 9-2 run over the first 2:05 of the fourth, but Rivers responded by sending Garnett and Allen back into the game — just to make sure nothing funny happened.

Arenas, now hearing a steady run of "your shooting is as good as your predictions" from the crowd, fouled Pierce on a breakaway, giving the captain a three-point play and the Celtics an 86-68 lead with 8:25 left.

Arenas finished with 21 points but shot 5-of-20 to get there.

Agent Zero's gutted prediction aside, his teammates were able to see the light.

"It's one game, but you know they're a force to be reckoned with," Caron Butler said. "With KG over there now, you know you have to tip your cap to them."

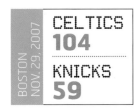

Kendrick Perkins slams the ball during the Celtics' crushing victory over the visiting New York Knicks. MATT STONE, BOSTON HERALD

CELTS' 45-POINT ROUT NEARS TEAM RECORD

>Mark Murphy, *Boston Herald*
November 30, 2007

TNT hadn't deemed it necessary to showcase a Celtics game in Boston since 2003, and even Doc Rivers knew what that meant.

"The last time we were on TNT, Danny Ainge was doing the game," the Celtics coach said last night of his boss, the former color analyst who actually brought Rivers to Boston just more than four years ago.

So with a national audience peering in on cable, appearances were important. The Knicks, apparently, didn't get the memo.

The Celtics followed the hype onto their biggest stage of the season, running their home record to 8-0 with a wild 104-59 win over the Knicks that was so overwhelming, not a single New Yorker reached double figures until Nate Robinson's meaningless 3-pointer at the buzzer.

"Boston came out with a playoff-type intensity, a national television game, and we didn't respond to that type of energy, and it's disappointing," Knicks coach Isiah Thomas said. "We're not ready for prime time yet, that's for sure."

Thanks to Robinson's shot, New York was spared the wrong kind of immortality. His bomb pushed the Knicks over the franchise low of 58 points, set on Dec. 15, 2000, against the Utah Jazz. The Knicks also just missed becoming the lowest-scoring Celtics opponent in the shot clock era, leaving the burden on a Milwaukee team that scored only 57 points on Feb. 27, 1955, in Providence.

"Of course I am embarrassed. We lost by nearly 50 points," Knicks guard Stephon Marbury said. "I'm angry. I'm always angry when I lose, but that was just flat-out embarrassing. To lose that bad was just ridiculous."

The Celtics' lead hit the 50-point mark (93-43) on an Eddie House trey with 7:48 left and flirted with the franchise record — a 51-point win (153-102) over Philadelphia on March 7, 1962 — the rest of the way. The hosts led by as many as 52 before falling back to 45 — all of it in extended garbage time. It still was the sixth-biggest win in franchise history.

And for a team that flew to Miami after last night's game in order to play the Heat tonight, the early blowout provided another bonus.

Kevin Garnett (23 minutes, eight points, 11 rebounds), Paul Pierce and Ray Allen (29 minutes and 21 points each) all received an early rest.

"Going into a back-to-back situation, it's ideal to spread the minutes around like that," Allen said.

After an early surge that produced a 54-31 halftime lead — with a 10-point first quarter from Rajon Rondo and a 16-2 run during the first seven minutes of the second essentially giving them all they needed — it was difficult for the C's not to desire more.

And here, once again, is where the Celtics sound like they have been reading the teachings of Bill Belichick.

"We were up big at halftime, but we told each other it wasn't about the score — it was about getting better," Pierce said. "You know, at one point I didn't even know we were up by 40 points. It was about us going out there, executing and getting better, because we're looking at this in the long run."

No offense was apparently taken.

"I don't think they were running the score up," said Quentin Richardson, who had seven points on 3-of-12 shooting for New York. "They were making shots, and we weren't. They held the ball there in the end, and Doc, he's a classy guy. They didn't try to put the score up or anything."

With fans shouting for the Celtics to push for the 50-point margin near the end, however, the margin was hard to ignore.

"Any time you play like that and you're up by 10 or 15, sometimes you let your guard down," Allen said. "That's why when we were up by 20 I didn't want to let up. We've had a lot of games this year where we were leading by 20 and it suddenly dropped to 10. It's a big lesson for the bench."

Not to mention the opponent.

REGULAR SEASON

Paul Pierce muscles his way toward the goal against Lakers center Kwame Brown. Pierce led all scorers with 33 points. MARK J. TERRILL, AP IMAGES

PIERCE, CELTICS SHOW HOW WEST WAS WON

›Mark Murphy, *Boston Herald*

December 31, 2007

It was all about fashion last night, from the tight throwback shorts that the Lakers mercifully scrapped at halftime for something less restrictive to the broad bandage over Kevin Garnett's right eye.

An Andrew Bynum elbow opened up that cut, but Garnett pushed off getting stitched up until after the game. Something of far more importance was on the line — a 4-0 western road swing.

The Celtics blew out a previously hot Lakers team, 110-91, and Red Auerbach can rest in peace for at least one more game.

Lakers coach Phil Jackson, who entered the game tied with Auerbach for seventh on the all-time NBA regular-season wins list at 938, won't be breaking that deadlock at the Celtics' expense after all.

Not when Paul Pierce, on the way to 33 points, scores 10 straight over the last three minutes of the third quarter. Not when Ray Allen picks up the torch and buries three straight jumpers, including a 3-pointer, in the first 1:30 of the fourth. And not when Eddie House completes the 11-2 run with a pull-up trey.

The Celtics didn't miss a shot in that run, just as they didn't miss on this road trip. The club ran its current road winning streak to 8-0 in the process.

"It's an important win because it was a goal to go undefeated on this trip," said C's coach Doc Rivers, whose club is now an NBA-best 26-3. "We rarely look more than one game ahead, but this is something we really wanted to do. I think the atmosphere really helped our guys because we had just played a very hard game the night before (at Utah) and it sort of picked us up."

Pierce, coming off a 24-point second half Saturday against Utah and a season-high 37-point performance Thursday against Seattle, took over at both ends during the last three minutes of the third quarter last night. He scored 10 straight points and stole the ball three times during one tough four-possession stretch. That gave the Celtics an 82-66 lead after Derek Fisher had cut the advantage to six (72-66) on a 3.

Pierce, who also opened the second half with a trey, had a three-point play and a 3-pointer during the run.

"When Paul stepped up we were also able to get some stops that really turned things for us," said Allen. "We have a formula for making the team we play feel uncomfortable, and on the defensive end we just locked in."

The Lakers, who shot 38 percent from the field, got 22 points from Kobe Bryant on 6-of-25 shooting.

Early on, it was Tony Allen who provided the spark for the C's.

Starting in place of point guard Rajon Rondo (hamstring), Allen finished with a six-point first quarter and followed with another seven through the first 5:14 of the second, including a slashing drive that gave the Celtics a 45-28 lead with 6:46 to go. But that 17-point advantage boiled down quickly.

The Celtics didn't score for another four minutes, shooting 0-for-4 from the field, missing two free throws (both by Kendrick Perkins) and turning the ball over three times during one four-possession stretch.

The Lakers responded with a 10-0 run that included five straight points from Bryant, including a free throw fueled by Rivers' technical foul.

Bynum capped the run with a pair of free throws that was another source of consternation for the Celtics bench. Though Garnett was called for the foul, he was also the one who ended up with a gash over his right eye.

Garnett went to the locker room and returned just in time to see Pierce find his groove again.

He also got one last look at the Lakers' short throwback shorts, which had Rivers laughing after the win.

"I told Kobe I know from this point on that our generation had better bodies than yours, because that was horrible," Rivers said.

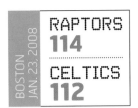
Paul Pierce reacts after
falling to the floor.
MATT STONE, BOSTON
HERALD

C'S CAN'T PUT A STOP TO IT

>Steve Bulpett, *Boston Herald*

January 24, 2008

The Celtics moved to 1-1 this week in holiday games with a 114-112 loss to the Raptors last night.

After beating the Knicks on Martin Luther King Day, they were toppled by Toronto on Switzerland Day.

Switzerland Day? Let's just say both clubs were conscientious objectors when it came to defense.

The Raptors shot 58 percent from the floor (15-for-21, 71.4 percent on 3-pointers), while the Celts had to miss their last two shots to fall under 50 percent.

Toronto was also helped immensely by the fact it made all 19 of its free throws.

The Celts saw their seven-point fourth quarter lead dwindle as the Raptors kept mixing in treys with their counterpunches.

With the margin down to three after a Kevin Garnett dunk with 1:10 left, Chris Bosh drove for a jam and, after a Paul Pierce miss, Jose Calderon hit two free throws to give Toronto four players with 20 or more points . . . and a 111-110 lead with 31.3 seconds remaining.

Eddie House then missed a trey from the right corner, but the ball came back out top to Ray Allen, who drilled a jumper with 14.9 left.

Calderon then drove the right side and scored while being fouled by Pierce. He made the free throw to put the C's down two with 10.5 on the clock.

House then missed from the right and Ray Allen couldn't squeeze in his follow-up attempt at a tie, leaving the Celts with their first loss to an Atlantic Division opponent in 11 outings.

The fact the Celtics went into the fourth quarter with a 91-84 lead is fairly amazing when you consider the damage the Raptors were doing to the strings.

After making all three of their treys in the second quarter, Toronto hoisted eight from long distance in the third and hot six of them. Carlos Delfino was 3-for-3 from beyond the arc in the new session, keeping the guests in a give-and-take situation with the lead — and there were nine lead changes in the quarter.

But the Celts weren't too shabby either from way out, making 4-of-5 in the quarter after bagging just 2-of-8 in the first half.

With Ray Allen hitting all four of his shots from the floor, the locals were warm from all over. They made 14-of-18 (77.8 percent) on all their field goals in the frame.

And whereas the Celtics managed to get three stops in the last 5 1/2 minutes of the third, the Raptors couldn't keep the C's from scoring on their last eight possessions.

Glen Davis went inside for a three-point play and Brian Scalabrine canned a 3-pointer with 0.7 seconds left to give the Celts a bit of breathing room at the three-quarter pole. The Celtics scored 29 points in the first quarter, but they can't be too proud of their output. It's not like the Raptors were playing a whole lot of effective defense.

The same could be said about the Celts, who surrendered 28 points.

With Garnett scoring 12 points on 5-for-7 shooting, the C's were a crisp 52.2 percent from the floor. But the Raptors got 10 points from Bargnani and were a bit better at 52.2 percent for the period.

The highlights for the C's were a pair of fast break alley-oop feeds from Ray Allen to Garnett for dunks.

The Celts appeared to be gathering steam when they went on a 9-2 run in the last few minutes. But Jose Calderon hit a jumper and Bosh made two free throws in the final 36 seconds to make it a one-point game.

Ray Allen drives past Cavaliers defender Devin Brown. Allen posted 20 points on 7-of-10 shooting against Cleveland.
TARA CARVALHO, BOSTON HERALD

RETURNS LOOK GOOD FOR CELTS

>Mark Murphy, *Boston Herald*
February 28, 2008

The "Boogie Fever Gino" video was put up on the Jumbotron with 2:49 left.

Times must be good again. The dancing fool — what passes this season for a human victory cigar — hadn't been unleashed for more than a month.

The Celtics last played a home game on Feb. 13, before Cleveland went through an extreme makeover.

But with the state of Ohio on higher alert than in Tuesday night's Democratic presidential debate after LeBron James turned his ankle in the second quarter, and with Zydrunas Ilgauskas battling extreme weight loss (eight pounds in two days) from an upper respiratory infection, the defending conference champions simply didn't have the legs last night.

Thus, the Celtics beat the radically remade Cavaliers, 92-87.

The result was possible despite a 12-point, 4-for-14 shooting, six-turnover performance from Paul Pierce. The Celtics captain has shot 19-for-51 (.373) from the field in four games against Cleveland this year, an interesting number if these teams meet in April or May.

It was possible despite the return of new Cavs Delonte West (season-high 20 points) and Wally Szczerbiak (12) to their old haunts.

It was possible despite a third-quarter dunk from James — resolutely back from his sprained ankle — that made him the youngest player in NBA history to cross the 10,000-point plateau at 23 years, 59 days. That's more than a year younger than Lakers star Kobe Bryant was when he hit the mark in 2003.

The result may not have been memorable, but with 26 regular-season games left and the best record (44-12) in the league still in hand, the Celtics were simply glad for a homecoming last night. "It's funny watching a game, being part of a game and then looking at the stats," coach Doc Rivers said of the Celtics' .523 shooting percentage, a number that climbed as high as 59 percent. "I didn't think we shot anywhere near 50 percent tonight. The pace of the game was real slow, so you don't think you're playing well offensively. But our defensive energy was good all night.

"Coming back from the West Coast, I was really concerned about this game. But I'm glad we were playing a team like Cleveland, because it forced us to have focus."

The necessary nudges came from players like Ray Allen (22 points on 7-for-10 shooting), Kevin Garnett (an 18-point, 11-rebound, five-assist, four-steal night) and Leon Powe and Glen Davis (combined 22 points and seven rebounds off the bench).

"(Tuesday) we said this was going to feel like a road game, and when you've been in the league long enough you know that first game feels like one of the toughest games," Garnett said. "It was just that. Our defense fueled us, gave us energy, made us talkative, and that was the difference at times."

Though the regular-season series between the two ended in a 2-2 tie, few doubt that Cleveland, with its massive changes that also include Ben Wallace, could make another visit here in April or May.

But last night the Cavaliers faded with barely a whiff of the stretch. Joe Smith hit a baseline jumper that cut the Cleveland deficit to nine points (75-66) before the Celts went into their finishing kick.

Starting with two Powe free throws, the hosts rolled out to an 84-68 lead with a 9-2 run that included four points from the hard-banging power forward.

Gino was the next order of business.

Kevin Garnett tangles with Detroit's Antonio McDyess. Garnett chipped in 31 points to lead all scorers in the victory for the Celtics.
JOHN WILCOX, BOSTON HERALD

C'S KISS 'EM GOODBYE

⟩Mark Murphy, *Boston Herald*

March 6, 2008

One can only imagine what late May — and the Eastern Conference finals — will be like if these two teams are still playing each other.

Celtics guard Ray Allen, after shooting the East to victory last month in the All-Star Game, had the conditions laid out by the Detroit Pistons' Rasheed Wallace.

"When we left (New Orleans), Rasheed said, 'Thanks for winning me the money I got, but now you can kiss me where the sun don't shine,'" said Allen, who, thankfully, didn't have to work on his playoff pucker last night at the Garden.

From an offensively channeled Kevin Garnett, who scored a season-high 31 points, to Kendrick Perkins and his career-high 20-rebound performance, to a full-scale push from Rajon Rondo, all involved helped the Celtics get past their chief competition in the conference last night in a 90-78 victory over Detroit.

The Celtics, a 24-win team last season, thus became the first team in the NBA to clinch a playoff spot last night. The Atlantic Division leaders, winners of six straight, will be making their first postseason appearance in three years.

An overpowering finish followed an 18-point third quarter by old friend Chauncey Billups that brought the Pistons to within two points entering the fourth. Detroit tied the game to open the final period on a Tayshaun Prince basket, before the C's regained the lead for good in a game in which they never trailed.

"Last year it would have been a parade," coach Doc Rivers said.

This year? The Celtics are now fishing for tuna instead of mackerel.

"It was a huge game for us and we knew it from Day One," Garnett said. "This is not an easy matchup. This is probably the deepest (team), not just because of the depth on the bench and stuff, but just because they are experienced."

The interesting part now, according to Rivers, is that his own team doesn't need to look to a result like last night's for an extraordinary amount of confidence.

"We already have a pretty confident bunch here," Rivers said.

Witness Rondo, after being on the receiving end of most of Billups' third-quarter drives and jukes, which the Detroit guard converted into 11-for-11 free throw shooting as the main part of his bid to win the game, flying in for a tomahawk dunk and hitting the floor following a rough, nothing-comes-easy foul from Pistons forward Jason Maxiell.

The Celts concluded the matter with a 13-0 run over the game's final 5:12.

"You don't want to take anything away from the Pistons," Paul Pierce said. "You don't want to get too overconfident against them. I remember in 2002 we were 3-1 or 4-0 against the New Jersey Nets and lost to them in the Eastern Conference finals. It's great to beat them in the regular-season matchup and win the series, but this is a team we're probably going to have to see in the playoffs. They'll be a better team by then."

If Pierce is as well-rested as last night, when he came in to hit two big shots in the game-ending run, the Celtics will be just as improved.

The Celtics captain, working on a 15-point night that included the team's only three 3-pointers, came up with the game's big steal when he picked off a Wallace pass, kicked the ball out to Rondo and took it back for the fast-break hoop and an 85-77 lead with 2:53 left, forcing a Detroit timeout. The basket came in the middle of a withering 13-0 run, which included a push by Rondo (16 points) for a three-point play and a Pierce trey.

"I pretty much just closed my eyes and the ball slipped out of my fingers and went in," Pierce said. "The shot clock was winding down and Kevin got me the ball and set a nice screen, and I saw nothing but daylight so I took the shot."

By the time Garnett hit Perkins (10 points) with a bullet pass and the center turned the feed into a 90-77 lead with 1:29 left, the run was over and so were the Pistons.

Seattle's Johan Petro battles Celtics teammates P.J. Brown and Glen Davis for a loose ball. MATT STONE, BOSTON HERALD

CELTS LOWER BOOM VS. NOT-SO-SUPER SONICS

》Steve Bulpett, *Boston Herald*
March 13, 2008

REGULAR SEASON

The physics did not look good for the Seattle SuperSonics last night. Playing the finale of a seven-game road trip, they had lost five straight and 9-of-10 while the Celtics arrived at the Garden with nine straight wins in their duffel bag ... and it was Kevin Garnett bobblehead doll night.

Is it really any surprise the SuperSonics wound up as merely the latest bug on the windshield of the large green wagon?

The 111-82 C's victory was as humane as the local entry could make it. While the people in sneakers ran out to leads as great as 37 points, the game presentation staff chose not to rub it in. Human victory cigar "Gino" didn't dance his way onto the videoboard until the 2:38 mark of the fourth quarter, when, in all reality, this one was over almost before the national anthem ended.

The regulars were on the bench in full relaxation mode for the fourth quarter as their close friends put a bow on the first 10-game winning streak (after two nine-gamers and an eight-game run) of the season. The C's have now won 11 in a row at home.

Bringing a Garnett doll with him into the postgame press meeting, Paul Pierce said, "I knew we couldn't lose when I saw that."

Or when he saw the Sonics.

Ray Allen hit 8-of-10 shots on the way to 18 points against his former team, while Garnett matched Allen's total and Pierce tossed in 14. Points simply weren't going to be an issue against a Seattle outfit that had given up an average of 115.8 points in its previous four games. The Celtics, on the other hand, had won their previous five by an average of 15.8.

In that the Sonics are in the process of blowing their team up and going young while the Celts are packing for a long playoff trip, mismatch doesn't begin to describe this exercise.

The Celts led by 10 after one quarter, 20 after two and 32 after three.

"Coach (Doc Rivers) said that he didn't have no great speech for us," Pierce said. "This is a game we should win, so let's go out there and handle business. And after those first couple of minutes, we did and pretty much put the game away in the first half."

Pierce was the biggest factor of the first quarter, scoring 14 points as the C's survived the indignity of a 19-17 deficit and stepped on the gas. A full bench complement was on the floor when the hosts did their most impressive first-half damage.

"I thought our bench is what changed the game," Rivers said. "The starting unit in the first six or seven minutes was good, but the second unit came in and they were great."

Eddie House had made just 14-of-50 shots in his last seven games, but he went 5-for-5 vs. Seattle for 11 points. Five assists gave House 22 in the last four games. James Posey contributed 10 points and the group as a whole provided the necessary defensive pressure to keep any foolish thoughts of a comeback out of the Sonics' heads.

"Nice professional win by our guys," said Rivers, who's been using that adjective quite a bit of late. "(The Sonics were playing) the seventh game on a hellish road trip, and our guys came out with great energy and took advantage of that."

In the end, it was a laugher — all the way to the dressing room.

"Get back on defense," said Pierce to the Garnett doll, giving it a whack while its model sat beside him.

"Paul Pierce, ladies and gentlemen," said Garnett as Pierce continued to play with his new toy.

Thank you. They'll be here all season and, they hope, well into June.

Boston Celtics guard Rajon Rondo — who scored 14 points, grabbed six rebounds and dished six assists — penetrates against Suns center Shaquille O'Neal. MATT STONE, BOSTON HERALD

PIERCE, CELTICS PUT BRAKES ON PHOENIX

》Mark Murphy, *Boston Herald*
March 27, 2008

REGULAR SEASON

When Paul Pierce took only six shots last Monday, he said he was merely going with the flow of the offense.

The Celtics captain also knew that a month ago, after shooting 2-for-13 during the Celtics' loss in Phoenix, he had just played his worst game of the season.

Say no more. The Suns had no hope of seeing the same Pierce again last night.

The Celtics split the season series with a 117-97 win over Phoenix at the Garden, building the national appetite for a potential NBA Finals matchup, and giving Pierce some nationally televised exposure. But it's funny how amnesia works.

"I really never think about my last games, truthfully," said a beaming Pierce. "Once it happens it's behind me. I'm one of the most confident players in this league. I could miss 100 shots and think the next one is going in."

His 27-point performance, including an explosive 12-point, 5-for-5 fourth quarter, set everything else in motion against a Suns team that was relegated to one fast-break basket. Phoenix, second in the league in scoring offense with an average of 110.1 points per game, has yet to score 100 points against the Celtics. They averaged 91 points over two games against a Celtics team that leads the league in scoring defense (90.04 ppg).

With Pierce and Kevin Garnett (30 points, 12-19 shooting) taking care of the offensive load last night, and with Rajon Rondo neutralizing Steve Nash, the Celtics dictated the pace against one of the most uncontrollable forces in the league.

"They are a great team, one through 12," said Suns center Shaquille O'Neal. "Against a team put together like this you have to do almost everything right, especially in this building."

Though Phoenix' new power axis of O'Neal (16 points) and Amare Stoudemire (32 points, 11-for-16) carved out early success in the paint, the Suns' better-known half — one of the game's most prolific running games — never reached the fast line.

"Every shootaround (assistant coach Tom Thibodeau) and Doc (Rivers) stress that we have to get back," Garnett said. "The time we played them down there they got a lot of fast-break points, but that was something we had to change."

The Celtics' ball-hawking also paid off. As Suns coach Mike D'Antoni bemoaned, his team was done in by 21 turnovers, with Stoudemire, O'Neal and Raja Bell combining for 13.

The Celtics converted those 21 miscues into 30 points, while also keeping their own mistakes (14) relatively low.

"The thing I was most happy with was that at halftime (Phoenix) was shooting 62 percent, and you could hear the guys saying, 'We need to do this, and we need to do that,' and I said 'We need to do what we've done all year,'" Rivers said. "We're making no changes. I was very stern about that. We're going to play our defense. They did that in the second half, and were great at it."

Pierce and Garnett took care of the rest with some powerful closing offense.

The C's, with the help of a four-point play from James Posey and a baseline jumper from Garnett with two seconds left in the quarter, carried an 84-73 edge into the fourth. Pierce then responded with his big fourth quarter that included two three-point plays and an unstoppable stroke at the expense of everyone who tried to guard him, including Grant Hill, Gordon Giricek and Bell.

Eddie House, who played the entire fourth, locked away the result with back-to-back 3-pointers, the second for a 110-88 lead and essentially the game with 4:36 left.

Ray Allen dunks during Boston's victory against Atlanta. Celtics' starters enjoyed an easy night in the rout.
LISA HORNAK, BOSTON HERALD

CELTS WON'T BUCK TREND

›Mark Murphy, *Boston Herald*

April 12, 2008

The Celtics had Gabe Pruitt making a rare appearance with nine minutes left and Glen Davis line driving home an improbable 18-foot jump shot.

Sam Cassell, back after a two-game absence, was the crunch-time point guard and the starters waited patiently on the bench for the nightly airing of Gino's victory dance.

The Celtics obviously don't make the same mistake twice.

Faced with a combative Bucks team Tuesday night in Milwaukee, the Celtics bench needed to go to overtime for a win.

Last night the Celtics improved on their act with a 102-86 win over the Bucks for their 63rd victory of the season.

The Celtics are now a remarkable 36-1 against sub-.500 teams, which goes a long way toward explaining why they have the best record in basketball.

"We play for ourselves, not other teams," said Kevin Garnett. "That's what (coach) Doc Rivers says to us. That comes to life when we play teams that don't have any significance.

"We tend to not play to the competition's level, because we are playing for the postseason. We must experience the reps. If we go in thinking we have to take care of business, and give other players the chance to play, we need nothing more and nothing less."

None of the starters played more than 25 minutes — the amount logged by Ray Allen — and none scored more than Rajon Rondo, who despite low minutes (23) still walked off with a 16-point, 10-assist double-double.

Instead, this marked yet another night for the bench to develop its playoff rhythm, with Cassell in particular jumping on the opportunity.

The point guard with the classic mid-range game finished with 10 points, four assists and four rebounds in 17 minutes. He also shot a solid 5-for-10 from the floor,

looking very much at home with the reserve unit he will be expected to lead in the playoffs.

"I actually thought Sam was big in that — keeping the team together," Rivers said.

Overall the numbers were truly bizarre, with the Bucks attempting 25 more free throws (30-5), making 17 more (21-4), and still losing by 16 points. Milwaukee also outworked the Celtics on the offensive glass (17-11).

But defense, as usual, was all the Celtics needed to close this game out. The most telling number was in shots. The Celtics made 13 more hoops (44-31) and attached a near-absurd 33 assists.

The Celtics were on their way into the stratosphere with a 25-point third-quarter lead (72-47) when the Bucks finally dug in. Milwaukee scored the next six points and after Cassell interjected with a 10-footer, Michael Redd hit his third 3-pointer of the night.

But the Bucks could only trade baskets for the rest of the quarter, with James Posey finally polishing off the third with a 3-pointer for a 79-58 Celtics lead.

By the fourth quarter the game had completely slipped away from the Bucks, with Rivers going quickly to his reserves.

It was Cassell's turn, in particular, to shine. And overall, it was time to show the rest of the league that regardless of the opponent, the Celtics are particularly good at looking straight ahead.

They don't lapse against the insignificant teams, as Garnett calls them.

"We did what we know we are capable of doing — just keeping it simple," Allen said. "It hasn't been a problem all year. We just have to make the simple pass. Offensively we have a lot of talent. Sometimes you get bogged down doing the mundane things, but it's important that you follow the script and make the easy play."

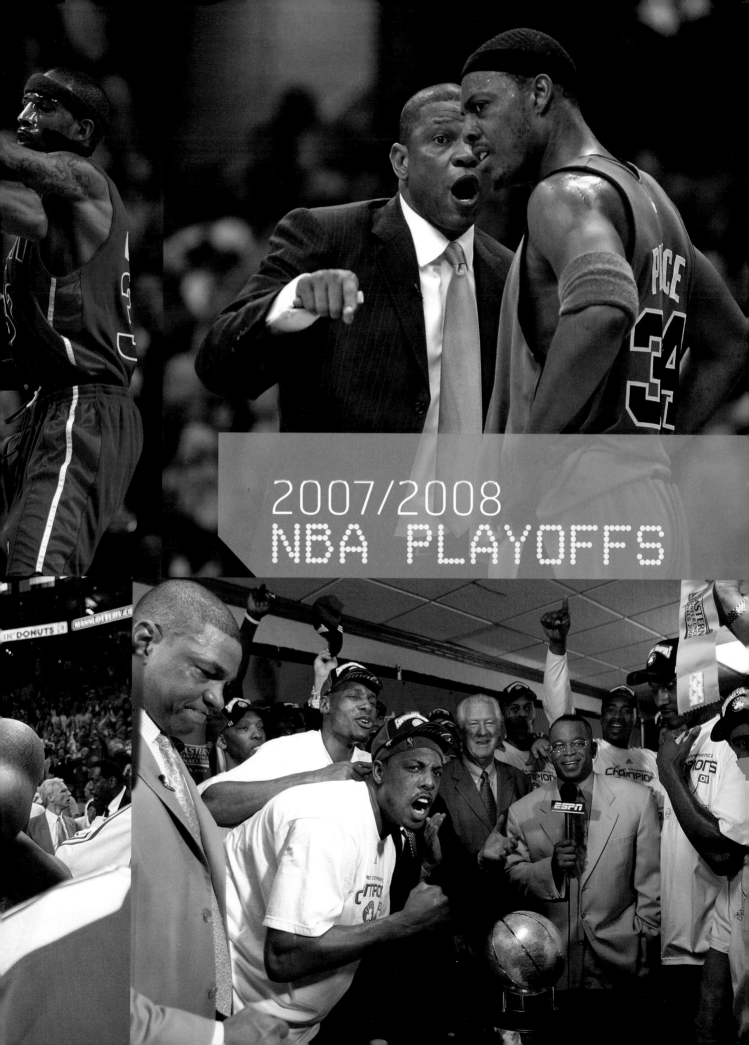

2007/2008
NBA PLAYOFFS

BOSTON
APRIL 20, 2008

CELTICS
104

HAWKS
81

Below: Rajon Rondo, who scored 15 points and recorded nine assists, looks to make a pass during the second half of the team's series-opening win against Atlanta. MATT STONE, BOSTON HERALD

Opposite: Kevin Garnett reacts to Leon Powe's slam dunk in the fourth quarter of the Celtics' victory against the Hawks. Lowe had 10 points. MATT STONE, BOSTON HERALD

WAIT LIFTED FROM CELTS

> Mark Murphy, *Boston Herald*

April 21, 2008

The night started with a smoky pyrotechnics display that didn't have a prayer of matching the heat from what followed.

Rajon Rondo hit everything from 20-footers to off-balance runners — one just before slamming onto his back. Ray Allen went on a one-man 10-4 rampage. David Ortiz got the assist on Lucky the Leprechaun's dunk.

The combination didn't matter. Everything worked like German engineering. The Celtics opened the NBA playoffs with a 104-81 win over Atlanta last night in Game 1 of their Eastern Conference first-round series at the Garden, and they haven't been better against the Hawks.

And there might be cause for worry because of that.

Any more excitement, and Kevin Garnett might start tickling the crowd or giving noogies to teammates.

Witness KG's reaction once Leon Powe punctuated the win by lunging through the outstretched arms of Josh Smith and Mike Bibby for a dunk with 5:57 left.

Powe, who drew the foul and went on to hit the free throw for a game-wrapping 23-point margin (91-68), ended up on his back.

And the jubilant Garnett, with the help of Sam Cassell, ended up on top of him, mercilessly jabbing the second-year forward in the chest.

"Leon is like a (grown) man," Garnett said of whether he was worried about losing control. "Those were like high-fives to him, except that he got it in the chest."

Allen nodded.

"Leon is probably the strongest guy on the team, so he probably didn't even feel it," he said.

Powe then replied: "Yeah, I didn't feel it — I was just talking to him. I was juiced, happy. Kevin was like a little kid.

Left: Ray Allen, who scored 18 points as one of six Celtics who hit double figures, moves past Hawks forward Josh Smith. MATT STONE, BOSTON HERALD

Opposite: Rajon Rondo took the Hawks out of their game by neutralizing Atlanta point guard Mike Bibby on defense and staying aggressive on offense. MATT STONE, BOSTON HERALD

He was just saying, 'That's what I'm talkin' bout.'"

Indeed, everything seemed infectious last night. Six Celtics hit double figures, including Powe and Cassell with 10 each off the bench. Four starters scored at least 15 points, with Allen's 18 leading the way.

Rajon Rondo, in perhaps the most anticipated matchup of the night, thoroughly outplayed the man who has tied the Hawks together into a cohesive unit — Mike Bibby.

Rondo finished with 15 points on 6-of-9 shooting from the field, nine assists and six rebounds. He also applied enough pressure to frustrate Bibby, who had just one assist, marking the first time in 52 career playoff games that he dished out less than two.

But beware, said captain Paul Pierce, thinking back to the last time the C's were in the playoffs during the 2004-05 season against Indiana.

"I remember the last time in the playoffs that we won Game 1 and lost the series," Pierce said. "So you don't know. You can't look at Game 1 as the indicator. We're not overconfident."

They are, however, in a secure place.

Per usual, they defended well, particularly in the second half, and limited the Hawks to 38 percent shooting. As evidenced by the shooting performances of Bibby (five points, 2-for-10), Joe Johnson (19, 7-for-22), Smith (six, 3-for-10) and Marvin Williams (nine, 2- for-7), nothing came easy.

The Celtics took their first 20-point lead (78-58) with 9:32 left in the game on Powe's back-cutting reverse layup.

From there, the margin kept rising like the price of oil. The price of oil, of course, could some day plummet.

"We'll take the win, but we did some things I know we can do better at both ends of the floor," coach Doc Rivers said. "We can play better, and that's the good news."

RAJON RONDO

Celtics' Rajon Rondo brimming with confidence

>Mark Murphy, *Boston Herald*

April 23, 2008

He always has been considered bright beyond his years, and certainly smarter than the rest of the people on the floor.

If the best basketball players see the game develop at a slower speed, then that was Rajon Rondo from the time he became a point guard.

"He's so smart," said Doug Bibby, who coached the Celtics point guard for three years at Louisville (Ky.) Eastern High School, before Rondo moved on to Oak Hill Academy in Virginia. "I pick his brains right now whenever I get the chance."

Everything about the energetic, wiry guard spoke of something from a higher level.

Bibby saw the game against Detroit earlier this season when Rondo drove home a Celtics win with a spectacular dunk over Jason Maxiell.

Compared to the confident high school star who could do everything well — from point guard, to quarterback, to a natural ability to excel in the classroom — Bibby saw nothing in that dunk that was a revelation.

"His sophomore year we ran an alley-oop for him, and he dunked on a guy's shoulders," said Bibby. "He was literally over the guy's shoulders."

Rondo also moved in rarefied circles at a young age. Bibby took Rondo out to Sacramento to meet his famous cousin, Kings point guard Mike Bibby, who now runs the offense for the Hawks. They shot around together and Rondo absorbed everything from the unusual opportunity.

The two are presently locked in a first-round NBA playoff series as opposing starters. Back in high school, Rondo undoubtedly foresaw this moment, or something like it.

"It's just not me," Rondo recently said with a shrug of whether he's ever been awed.

That attitude is made to order for someone asked to man the point for Kevin Garnett, Paul Pierce and Ray Allen this season. Someone with a lesser sense of self wouldn't have managed nearly as well.

When the majority of the NBA rightly pointed to Rondo as the Celtics' major issue six months ago, the large chip on his shoulder wasn't taken into consideration.

He expected to succeed.

"He's heard naysayers all year, and I told him that you don't answer them, except to play," Celtics coach Doc Rivers said. "If I had tried to answer all of those people, I would have been gone years ago."

CHANGING PERCEPTIONS

Just before a game not so long ago, Garnett pulled up a chair in front of Rondo in the locker room and started to talk, and talk. The younger player said little.

His eyes were trained on Garnett's, occasionally nodding his head, but otherwise simply absorbing the wisdom. It's difficult to imagine Rondo, who appears to be as malleable as clay, came out of college with the tag of being uncoachable.

He finds it hard to believe as well, but that was indeed the perception — that Rondo, after two frustrating years of attempting to adapt his open court game to Tubby Smith's

Rajon Rondo's increased maturity, which he gained from listening to his more mature, experienced teammates, made him an instrumental part of the 2008 World Champion Celtics squad. MATT STONE, BOSTON HERALD

THE TEAM

more deliberate system at Kentucky, was too bull-headed.

If there's something that can get even a minor rise out of Rondo, it's that accusation. But he had to live with it. After leaving Kentucky following his sophomore season, Rondo had to answer the question from every general manager he met.

"I don't really know how it came up," he said. "There was one game at Kentucky where I got benched, and I guess it might have come from that. It wasn't just me. There were a couple of starters. One day a team was kicking our butts, and me and Randolph Morris were taken out of the lineup.

"I don't know if that hurt me in the draft, but people interviewed me. I was asked that by a couple of teams."

The Celtics, too, were aware of this rap, though Danny Ainge ultimately was undeterred in his decision to pass up taking a guard higher in the first round of the 2006 draft. He instead traded for Phoenix' pick at No. 21 and took Rondo.

"That's the sort of thing that we do check into," Ainge said. "I had heard that he was a difficult kid to coach. I watched Rajon, and I could tell that he wasn't on the same page with his college coach. He wasn't listening to what his college coach was saying. I think it was a lot of things that went into it — a little bit of it was intensity, but he wasn't playing the way that he wanted to.

"I saw what I saw, I knew some of the issues, and I didn't think there was anything that was uncorrectable. There was a great talent in Rajon. We were confident after meeting with him that we could get along. Doc has done a great job of coaching Rajon, and that's what coaching is.

"He's matured a lot with the coaching, and understanding the difference between being coached and being criticized," Ainge said.

To this day Rondo insists he is friends with Tubby Smith. The friction wasn't personal. Part of the trouble simply stemmed from that intelligence — the unwavering confidence he knew as well as anyone else how to play the game. Kentucky wasn't the only place where Rondo was benched. Bibby admits Rondo arrived at Eastern High with a sizable attitude about his own abilities.

"I had to bench him in some games," Bibby said. "There were some things I didn't agree with. In the beginning it can be hard enough going from middle school to high school. But it's not that I thought Rajon was uncoachable. He just wanted to win."

Bibby was more inclined to listen when, after pulling Rondo to the side during a dispute, the guard pointedly talked back.

"I remember one time we got into it, and I said, 'Rajon, remember that I'm the one who feeds the floor,' " he said. "And he said 'Coach, I'm the one on the floor.' I had to step back and think about that for a moment."

QUICK DEVELOPMENT

He still talks back, as evidenced by an oncourt argument with Ray Allen over an inbounds pass during a recent game in Chicago. Allen respected Rondo's chutzpah, as well as the young guard's apology upon realizing that he was wrong.

The process continues.

"He's not easy, but he's better than he was," Rivers said. "He's a kid with a great basketball IQ and stubbornness, and those things get in the way sometimes.

"There's a difference between individual and team knowledge. I'm sure that got him in trouble in Kentucky, and it's been that way here at times."

What few outside of the Celtics locker room saw coming was the influence of an All-Star lineup on such rapid development by Rondo.

"Clearly," Rivers said. "Put any of these guys next to Kevin, Ray and Paul and it will help them. But when someone speaks up you can't take it personally, and he doesn't. He's had disagreements with the Big Three at times. But I've told them all that you have to stand up for yourself."

At least now the setting is right.

"They make it easy," Rondo said of his celebrated company. "It was not easy last year. It was different because we had a lot of young point guards. My only vet was Paul. But I listen. I have an open mind. I still voice my opinion a lot, but I don't look at everything as the coach criticizing me. I got my thick skin last year, because I was a rookie, and I had to take everything."

Besides, Rondo finally has realized that at least on this level, many more see the game at the same speed.

"He sees a lot of what you don't see," Rondo said of playing for a former point guard. "I have an advantage in that way. On one play (last week) I made a mistake, and he just said, 'Keep your chin up, the next time you'll make the right decision.'

"I know I have a long way to go, but I can still see the play before it happens."

BOSTON
APRIL 30, 2008

CELTICS
110

HAWKS
85

Left: Sam Cassell (left) celebrates with teammate Kendrick Perkins during Game 5 action. Cassell came off the bench to score 13 points in 15 minutes. MATT STONE, BOSTON HERALD

Opposite: Paul Pierce struggles for control of the ball. Pierce contributed a team-high 22 points in the win. MATT STONE, BOSTON HERALD

GARDEN PARTY FOR C'S

>Mark Murphy, *Boston Herald*

May 1, 2008

It all came back to them with the change in latitude, as if cooler weather was needed to drive Atlanta's shooting back down to the depths, and their own fortune back onto a hot plate.

Paul Pierce, Kevin Garnett and Ray Allen all took their star turns, with key fill-ins supplied by Sam Cassell, James Posey and an absolutely thunderous Leon Powe.

The Celtics, faced with a frantic public and a brave opponent, nailed down Game 5 and their third win of the series last night with a 110-85 roll over the Hawks. Though Joe Johnson was again tough, this time with 21 points, the Hawks were relegated to the frustrating role of chaser. They shot 40.6 percent, a number very much in line with their efforts in Games 1 and 2.

The Celtics, at 53.6 percent, couldn't miss.

Led by Pierce's 22-point, six-assist, seven-rebound assault — clearly his best performance of the first-round affair — the Celtics took a 3-2 series lead with the knowledge that anything less would have pushed 18,624 doubters out onto Causeway Street.

Cassell, whose 13-point, 6-for-8 performance was one of his best since joining the Celtics on March 4, shook his head at the thought of all those worriers. "No panic in the locker room," he said. "We're just taking care of our home court. This is why we work so hard in the regular season — to get that."

The puzzle is why the Celtics, despite a league-leading 31-10 road record during the regular season, once again

Below: Ray Allen relaxes before the start of Game 5. MATT STONE, BOSTON HERALD

Opposite: Boston's Leon Powe collides with Atlanta's Zaza Pachulia. Powe grabbed seven rebounds and scored 10 points off the bench. MATT STONE, BOSTON HERALD

fly into Atlanta for tomorrow night's Game 6 with the queasy thought that they have yet to win a road game in the playoffs.

"So much focus was put on our defense, but Joe Johnson made plays," Garnett said of Games 3 and 4. "We fought for home court for a reason, but he made plays when he had to."

The difference was that Johnson was largely alone last night. Josh Smith, despite 18 points that was held up by 10-for-10 shooting from the line, shot 4-for-13 from the floor. Marvin Williams was 4-for-10, and Mike Bibby contracts the flu whenever he comes to Boston.

The Hawks point guard, who had two career playoff-low, one-assist performances in Games 1 and 2, had his third one-assist game of the series last night. He also had a familiar shooting line — 2-for-8 for six points. Numbers dropped in the other end, too. Smith, who set a franchise playoff record with seven blocks in Game 4, only had one last night.

With the Hawks running on a low ebb, Pierce started quickly with a 10-point first quarter and never stopped. Rajon Rondo (12 points, seven assists) broke the Hawks down immediately, and Powe, with 10 points and seven

first-half boards, created mayhem in the paint.

The Celtics were particularly porous in the paint during their two losses in Atlanta.

In Game 4 the Celtics also blew a 10-point fourth-quarter lead. Last night they started the same juncture with a 17-point edge (81-64), courtesy of 3-pointers form Allen and Posey and a three-point play from Pierce over the last 2:34 of the third quarter.

This time they were able to make their good work stick, starting with Posey's second trey one minute into the fourth.

By the time Garnett dunked with 8:58 left, the Celtics were ahead by 19 (89-70). The Hawks would have trouble moving beyond that margin the rest of the night.

"We have to do it again, and we have to do it on the road now," Celts coach Doc Rivers said. "It's going to be an amazing atmosphere down there, and we're going to have to go in and play like tonight. If the offense isn't as good as it was tonight, then we still have to win the game with our defense. The thing I liked is that both were good tonight. But at some point we have to win when our offense isn't as good, and our defense has to be great."

They may not have to wait long.

CELTICS
99
HAWKS
65

Below: Boston players (from left) Paul Pierce, Kendrick Perkins, Rajon Rondo, Ray Allen and Kevin Garnett
celebrate a Glen Davis dunk late in the fourth quarter.
MATTHEW WEST, BOSTON HERALD

Opposite: Kevin Garnett gets fired up during the Celtics'
Game 7 against the Hawks. STUART CAHILL, BOSTON HERALD

A MAGNIFICENT SEVEN

>Mark Murphy, *Boston Herald*

May 5, 2008

Kevin Garnett performed last rites with — typical for him — a gesture not intended for a family venue.

He laid the ball in with 3:04 left in the third, got pushed by Zaza Pachulia, and kept stumbling forward. Garnett abruptly pulled up and stared at the fans, made a slashing motion across his throat and said, "It's all over."

The Celtics were leading by 36 points (70-34) at that point. No amount of time was enough for the Hawks to recover. And they didn't. The C's kept pouring it on in a 99-65 win that was one of their biggest routs of the season.

The Celtics start their Eastern Conference semifinal series tomorrow night against Cleveland, and if they

don't understand how to finish off an opponent now, they never will.

No one, the Celts included, expected this series to go seven games, though they won't necessarily tell you that.

"I don't think it went longer than we expected," said James Posey, managing to keep a straight face. "They're a tough team."

Indeed, the 37-win Hawks were so tenacious that the Celtics were forced onto a meditation mat.

"Paul (Pierce) and Doc (Rivers) both said that we learned a lot about ourselves in this series," Garnett said

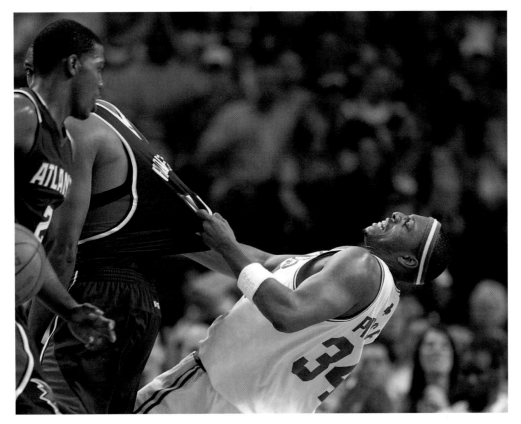

Left: Paul Pierce gives Al Horford's jersey a mighty tug as he reacts to being knocked down.
MATTHEW WEST, BOSTON HERALD

Opposite: Atlanta forward Marvin Williams was ejected for flagrantly fouling Rajon Rondo in the decisive Game 7.
MATTHEW WEST, BOSTON HERALD

of the team's captain and its coach. "If there's a message in there, it's that we play great defense, and we're very comfortable at home."

The Celtics responded yesterday with a level of defense no other team in the league has played this season. Before garbage time took hold in the fourth, the Hawks didn't hit 20 points in any of the first three quarters, including a 10-point second.

Atlanta's 26-point first half was a playoff record-low for a Celtics opponent. The Hawks shot 29.3 percent for the game, and also forked over 17 turnovers, which the Celtics converted into 27 points.

If the C's continue to defend this way, few will care when the offense goes into an occasional lapse.

"Absolutely," Garnett said of the role defense should play every night. "Just knowing my assignment, knowing I've got help on the back end, knowing that when I do what I'm supposed to do another guy is doing what he is supposed to do.

"I thought as far as communication that we were talkative — loud. We wanted to cut down on our fouls, we wanted to play defense with our feet and chests. I thought we did a good job of moving our feet, contesting shots and rebounding collectively."

All qualities that were lacking when they played in Atlanta.

But as yesterday's margin grew, those frustrating moments for the C's on the road fluttered away.

The Celtics hit their first 10-point lead (20-10) in the first quarter, their first 20-plus edge (47-26) when Pierce opened the third quarter with a 3-pointer, and their first 30-point edge (60-30) on a Garnett turnaround with 6:19 left in the third.

They were flirting with a 40-point lead (79-41) when the third ended, before the fourth-quarter free-for-all started to dilute the margin.

"The two biggest games we played in this series were our best — Games 5 and 7," Rivers said. "I think that a lot of players on this team have been through a lot of playoff games, but we haven't been through anything as a team. I thought this was important for us.

"The pressure from this will pay off later."

CELTICS
76

CAVALIERS
72

Below: Celtics head coach Doc Rivers disputes a foul call with an official during Game 1 of the NBA Eastern Conference Semifinals. MATTHEW WEST, BOSTON HERALD

Opposite: Paul Pierce had a tough night from the floor, but scored an easy two on a lay up over Cleveland center Ben Wallace and guard Delonte West. MATTHEW WEST, BOSTON HERALD

REINING KING

> Mark Murphy, *Boston Herald*

May 7, 2008

There isn't a defensive scheme that LeBron James hasn't seen, according to Doc Rivers. No rotation, no player, no two players, nothing that can be designed on a clipboard.

But the Celtics certainly did imitate and recycle until they turned virtually every drive into agony for the Cleveland star.

They simply ran the house at James last night — with Paul Pierce, James Posey and even both Allens (Ray and Tony) up front and lots of help underneath — and walked off with a 76-72 win against the Cavaliers in Game 1 of the Eastern Conference semifinals.

James, who missed his last five shots and was 1-for-8 in the fourth quarter, finished with an anomaly — a 12-point night on 2-for-18 shooting with 10 turnovers. He averaged 29.8 points in his first six playoff games.

On the other side, Kevin Garnett, oft-criticized for his tendency to pass up shots in crunch time, produced two big hoops — a 20-footer and a wheeling hook — in the last 1:17 to go along with two free throws each from an energized Sam Cassell and Posey. Garnett had a game-high 28 points with eight rebounds and three assists, while Cassell's 10-point fourth quarter was one of his finest moments with the Celts.

The fact that this game pulled into the station with both teams in the 70s might be causing a throwback headache for some.

Ray Allen took only four shots and was scoreless in a playoff game for the first time in his career. Pierce, expending a greater share of his energy than usual at the defensive end, had four points on 2-for-14 shooting.

Left: Celtics forward Glen Davis battles for position on a rebound against Cavaliers forward Joe Smith.
MATTHEW WEST, BOSTON HERALD

Opposite: Kevin Garnett shoots over the Cavaliers' Ben Wallace. Garnett finished with a game-high 28 points.
MATTHEW WEST, BOSTON HERALD

There could be a trend here, the sort that would make two of Rivers' former coaches, Pat Riley and Mike Fratello, happy.

"I thought this was the (old) Knicks-Heat series for about 20 minutes out there," Rivers, the C's coach, said of the slow, cumbersome pace, with the Cavs scoring 22 of their points from the free throw line and the C's turning the ball over 23 time. "Well, that was a beautiful win. I guess I'll put it that way."

But there were two ways to look at this one. Despite limiting Cleveland to 30.7 percent shooting and basically shutting down James, the C's still managed to win by only four. On the other hand, they won despite four total points from Pierce and Allen.

"If you're Cleveland, you're thinking you almost won with LeBron playing that way. And if you're us, you're thinking we won with Paul and Ray playing that way," Rivers said. "So it's probably a wash."

James, who had scored at least 30 in nine of his previous 10 games against the C's, was kept out of the paint for the most part.

The Celtics trailed by two (70-68) with 1:30 left when Garnett tied the game with his 20-footer. James missed with a stumbling scoop, and Cassell, after getting clocked by Zydrunas Ilgauskas, hit both freebies for a 72-70 lead.

James missed again, but Ilgauskas (22 points, 12 boards) put it back.

Garnett then wheeled past Joe Smith with a sweeping hook for a 74-72 lead with 21 seconds left. James, with Posey on him tight, missed his fifth straight shot on another makeable drive. Posey grabbed the board, was fouled, and hit both free throws for a 76-72 lead with 8.5 seconds left.

It was just enough to make some truly ugly basketball worthwhile.

"This was two heavyweights just body punching," Garnett said. "There was no finesse, no jabs, just all body punches, just an all-out, beat-down defensive fight."

KENDRICK PERKINS

C's Perk up on defense

›Mark Murphy, *Boston Herald*
May 8, 2008

One man's great defense can be another's accident.

When Cavaliers star LeBron James missed his last drive in Tuesday night's 76-72 Celtics victory over Cleveland in Game 1 of their Eastern Conference semifinal series at the Garden, much was made of Kendrick Perkins' ability to influence the play while also avoiding the foul.

The Celtics center looked limber and controlled, imposing enough to discourage one of the game's great shot-makers. But leave it to a coach to see the moment differently.

"I think, more than anything, that Perk got caught in that position and was just trying to get out of the way," Celtics coach Doc Rivers said yesterday at the team's practice facility. "It was more him being in that position and trying to disappear, thinking, 'Oh, please don't see me, please don't call the foul on me.'"

To illustrate his point, Rivers covered his head with his arms and cringed, as if he had just been cornered in a game of dodgeball.

The bottom line is that James missed and Perkins looked good, even in spite of himself. Last season, Perkins would have been called for the foul.

"Well, maybe," Perkins said. "You know what? I probably would have fouled him, honestly."

The center's growth, especially as a defensive player, is being recognized. When TNT requested a C's player to go on camera with Cheryl Miller yesterday, Perkins and point guard Rajon Rondo got the call.

When James attempted to drive off picks Tuesday night, Perkins was often the big man sealing off the gaps, 20 feet from the basket, sliding along the perimeter with the nimbleness of, well, Kevin Garnett.

"He's grown tremendously over the years, man," Paul Pierce said. "I don't know when the all-defensive team comes out, but if Perk isn't on it then I'll be surprised. I know KG is the defensive player of the year but he's got somebody next to him. The greatest thing about Kendrick is his understanding of his role. Kendrick could be an All-Star when you see what other centers are doing across the league. He could definitely be an All-Star."

When Game 2 tips off tonight at the Garden, Perkins will settle for matters that he can control, like the paint.

A season of playing next to Garnett has clearly sparked his game. The same is true of first-year assistant coach Tom Thibodeau's defensive rotations.

"I think I'm just understanding my role a whole lot better. It's that more than anything," Perkins said. "I've picked up a lot of things from Kevin, like how to guard against the pick-and-roll. Thibs takes his job very seriously. He gets here at 5 every morning and he doesn't leave until 8 every night. You have to trust someone who works that hard. You know he's going to put you in a position where you're going to succeed. He doesn't ask anything of you that you can't do." Growth may also be a matter of who is no longer on the scene.

"I really believe that a big part of this is having Garnett around," Rivers said. "Now Perk doesn't look at that position on the floor and think, 'I should be getting the same touches as him.' With Al (Jefferson) that's kind of how it went. It was the whole thing of being best friends, and out of that there was a natural kind of competition. With (Garnett) there's no question of who is going to get what.

"I think it was also kind of tough for Perk last year because he had to be the main defender back under the basket, and he was worried about someone having his back. He doesn't have that worry now. I'm just proud that he's had great focus while doing it."

That's good to know the next time Perkins spots James drawing a bead on the rim or about to burst off a pick.

"Hey, it's the playoffs," Perkins said. "I didn't expect to be dribbling the ball down the floor, either, but that's something I did (Tuesday) night."

Cleveland forward Wally Szczerbiak attempts a difficult shot over the outstretched hand of Kendrick Perkins.
MATTHEW WEST, BOSTON HERALD

THE TEAM

CAVALIERS
108

CELTICS
84

@ CLEVELAND
MAY 10, 2008

Below: Kevin Garnett, Rajon Rondo and Paul Pierce sit on the bench following the Celtics' Game 3 loss to Cleveland.   STUART CAHILL, BOSTON HERALD

Opposite: Sam Cassell falls to the ground while being guarded by Cleveland forward Joe Smith.
STUART CAHILL, BOSTON HERALD

ROAD WORRIERS: C'S OUT OF THEIR ELEMENT

> Mark Murphy, *Boston Herald*

May 11, 2008

This is officially a mystery. Send the Celtics on the road for a playoff game, and imposters show up on the other side.

Great defenders are replaced by a ragtag bunch who look as if they learned the game from Paul Westhead. Intensity is overcome by indecision.

The Celtics, presented with a chance to secure their first road win of the playoffs, instead fell from a first-quarter punch and barely got off the floor in last night's 108-84 loss to Cleveland.

The Cavaliers cut the Celtics' edge in this Eastern Conference semifinal series to 2-1, adding another chapter to the case against the Celtics as a capable playoff road team.

The C's couldn't even blame this one on a LeBron James comeback. The Cavaliers star didn't heat up until the second half — and even then only barely, finishing with 21 points on 5-for-16 shooting. Instead, the Celtics were attacked more directly by their itinerant former teammates. Delonte West (21 points, seven assists) and Wally Szczerbiak combined for 37 points, including six 3-pointers.

Left: Cleveland forward LeBron James is taken out with a hard foul by James Posey as Sam Cassell swats at the ball. STUART CAHILL, BOSTON HERALD

Opposte: Kevin Garnett sits on the bench, a towel over his head, late in the fourth quarter of Boston's 108–84 loss to Cleveland. AP IMAGES

James may have continued to miss shots, but his eight-assist performance pointed to his continued ability to make life easy for his teammates.

And this time the Celtics, on the way to a 40.5 percent shooting performance, simply didn't have enough going offensively to avoid their first playoff blowout loss. Kevin Garnett (17 points, nine rebounds) and Paul Pierce (14 points, 3-for-8) led a sorry attack.

The Celtics set all kinds of playoff lows in the first quarter — fewest points (13), worst shooting percentage (31.6) and most points by an opponent (32), as well as highest shooting percentage (65.0) by an opponent.

Nor did it get much better. The Cavaliers went on to shoot 53.6 percent — easily the highest by a Celtics opponent in 10 playoff games.

The Cavs' peak lead of 26 in the second quarter withered when the Celtics finally started to make an inroad in the third, cutting the deficit to 12 points (71-59) when Pierce hit two free throws with 3:17 left.

But with only a Kendrick Perkins free throw to interject, the Cavs hit back with an 8-2 closing run that included a deep trey and two free throws from James for a 78-60 lead. The Celtics barely dented that margin over the last 1:20 of the third, and Cleveland carried a 79-63 lead into the fourth quarter.

The Celtics would never get closer than that 12-point cushion.

The Celtics didn't need much to slip into their new, frustrating road persona.

The Cavs, courtesy of a 14-0 run, led by a 14-4 score after six minutes, 18-6 after 7:32 and 27-8 after 10 minutes.

With West hitting two 3-pointers and Szczerbiak and James sinking one each, the Cavs were making up for their offensive troubles in Boston all at once.

Cleveland walked out of the first quarter with a 32-13 lead.

Celtics point guard Rajon Rondo, continuing to struggle, was replaced by Sam Cassell nine minutes into the game, and by the second quarter, the bench — with the exception of Pierce — dominated the Celtics lineup.

The Cleveland-born James Posey stirred something up when he clotheslined James during a drive. As the Cavs star lay on his back, the Celtics forward was called for a flagrant foul.

Posey and Anderson Varejao, after being separated during a subsequent dispute, were also called for double technical fouls.

@ CLEVELAND
MAY 12, 2008

CAVALIERS
88

CELTICS
77

Below: Cleveland's LeBron James (center) yells at his mother, Gloria, who left her seat after a questionable foul on James by Paul Pierce, second from left. Boston's Kevin Garnett (right) tries to break up the family feud. AP IMAGES

Opposite: Cavaliers forward LeBron James penetrates against P.J. Brown. James finished with 21 points and 13 assists. STUART CAHILL, BOSTON HERALD

ROUGH ROAD FOR C'S

>Mark Murphy, *Boston Herald*

May 13, 2008

The gorilla on the Celtics' back is now the size of King Kong.

That winless weight the Celtics have carried on the playoff road just added a ton of urgency.

This time, the Celtics collapsed down the stretch, missing seven of their last nine shots and coughing up their lowest scoring quarter (12 points) of the playoffs in last night's 88-77 Game 4 loss to Cleveland.

The Eastern Conference semifinal series, now tied at 2, moves to the Garden tomorrow night — a game with huge implications.

On a night when the Cavaliers star had to tell his mother, Gloria, to sit back in her baseline seat after she started shouting at Paul Pierce following the Celtics captain's wrap-up foul of her son, LeBron James finally was able to add a little punctuation to his work.

His 21-point game, though not any more efficient than any previous ones, included two huge fourth-quarter hoops — a 3-pointer and a tomahawk dunk that deadened what spirit the C's had left.

Pierce scored six of his 13 points in the last 8:30 but also was a large part of the problem, missing three of his

Left: Ray Allen drives against Cleveland forward Joe Smith. Allen scored 15 points to lead the team. STUART CAHILL, BOSTON HERALD

Opposite: Celtics head coach Doc Rivers yells at Paul Pierce during a break in play. STUART CAHILL, BOSTON HERALD

last four shots.

James' second 3-pointer of the night gave the Cavs a 79-73 lead, and after Pierce followed with a driving, double-teamed banker, Daniel Gibson buried a deep trey for an 82-75 Cleveland lead.

Ray Allen missed a 20-footer, and James came back off the baseline with his most emphatic play of the series — a high-rising tomahawk dunk off the baseline for an 84-75 Cavaliers lead with 1:45 left.

The Celtics, who had missed six of their previous seven shots, continued to struggle when Pierce drove and missed a bank hook.

Anderson Varejao hit a 10-footer, and Pierce, forcing the issue all the way, finally connected to cut the Cavs' lead to 86-77.

But Varejao buried the final dagger, a 20-footer with 31 seconds left.

The Celtics trailed by two (45-43) at halftime and their deficit had slipped to three (68-65) by the end of the third quarter, though not because of poor shooting.

They broke through with their hottest quarter since

Game 2 but were countered by a nine-point period from Wally Szczerbiak and other assorted bombs, including a James 3-pointer. The lead changed hands 13 times, with Rajon Rondo and Allen — the latter with two 3-pointers — hitting stride.

Cleveland finally increased the pressure on a deep Gibson trey with 8:30 left for a 74-69 Cleveland lead. Though Pierce answered with a 12-footer, the next time down he forced a trey that missed wide. James made the Celtics pay with a drive and no-look pass to Joe Smith for the reverse layup and a 76-71 Cleveland lead with 7:27 to go.

The Celtics had their starters in place — with P.J. Brown replacing Kendrick Perkins — with 5:42 left and the Cavs leading by three (76-73). Brown had hit two big jumpers to help the cause, but as evidenced by three straight misses, getting closer would be a problem.

Someone was bound to break this scoreless stretch in a big way — with the Celtics missing four straight — and James blew it open with 3:18 left when his 3 gave the Cavs a 79-73 lead.

CELTICS
96

CAVALIERS
89

BOSTON
MAY 14, 2008

Below: Sam Cassell pleads his case with a referee after falling into fans' laps during Game 5 of the NBA semifinals. MATT STONE, BOSTON HERALD

Opposite: Paul Pierce dunks for two of his 29 points. MATT STONE, BOSTON HERALD

VICTORY GARDEN BLOOMS

>Mark Murphy, *Boston Herald*

May 15, 2008

Perhaps because they rarely were challenged during the season, the Celtics look so utterly flawed now.

But after last night's 96-89 win against Cleveland, this much is evident: The Celtics are going nowhere with their emotions left in the locker room.

The team that almost was too cool and uninvolved during two losses in Cleveland finally rediscovered its ability to explode with a defense-fueled, second-half charge.

Led by one of Rajon Rondo's best performances of the season — the point guard slashed for 20 points and 13 assists — the Celtics took a 3-2 series lead with a cathartic burst.

Kevin Garnett shook off the paralysis from a scoreless fourth quarter in Game 4 and surged for 26 points and 16 rebounds. Paul Pierce scored 10 of his 29 points in the fourth, and the Celtics withstood LeBron James' best shooting performance of the series.

The Cavaliers star scored 35 points on 12-for-25 shooting and appeared to be setting the stage for a special, domineering night with a 23-point first half.

"LeBron got to the paint way too much in the first half, and he was rejecting our pick-and-roll coverage," Celtics coach Doc Rivers said. "But we hadn't played well; LeBron had played great, and it was a (three)-point game at the half. I just believed that at some point we would play well. I believed coming into this series that we would have to win a game where he played great."

The glitterati were out in force for what started as a

Left: Boston's Glen Davis flips over the back of Cavaliers forward Wally Szczerbiak. MATT STONE, BOSTON HERALD

Opposite: Ray Allen crashes into fans during Game 5. MATT STONE, BOSTON HERALD

major statement game from James. Hip-hop star and Nets part-owner Jay-Z sat next to the Cavaliers bench while his bride, Beyonce, attempted to hide under the brim of a plaid golf hat across the floor from Celtics regular Donnie Wahlberg. Actors Rob Lowe and Jonah Hill ("Superbad") sat in one end zone, and the Patriots' Richard Seymour in the other. Even Antoine Walker, spotted in the front row, somberly held up a fist for the camera-linked Jumbotron.

In the irony of ironies, Walker, a longtime critic of Danny Ainge, was on hand when the Celtics director of basketball operations accepted his NBA Executive of the Year trophy.

Not that any of these sights were taken in by the Celtics. After two bad losses in Cleveland and an equally bad start last night, they needed blinders as well as an intensity boost.

Rondo, whom the Cavs once again dared to shoot, provided the latter with back-to-back 3-pointers during a 14-3 run late in the second quarter.

"That started our run going into halftime, and it carried into the third quarter," Pierce said. "We were able to get the lead and not relinquish it."

The Celtics actually took the lead four times in the third quarter before finally holding on. They shot a scorching 75 percent (12-for-16) in the period, including a 10-for-12 finish in the last 9:18 for a 72-63 lead.

Though they pushed out as far as 12 points (84-72) with 5:48 left in the game, finishing off the Cavs was difficult because of a slashing, kamikaze performance by Delonte West.

The former Celtics guard scored 11 of his 21 points in the fourth quarter, including seven from the line.

Two bad turnovers — one from James Posey and another from Ray Allen — led to West scores that left the Celtics up 91-87 with 45.5 seconds left.

Garnett missed a 15-footer at the shot-clock buzzer, but Allen tipped the rebound back to Garnett. Pierce was fouled and hit both free throws for a six-point edge with 15.6 seconds left. Despite two more West free throws, the C's held on just long enough.

CAVALIERS
74

CELTICS
69

Below: Kevin Garnett scraps for the ball with Cleveland's Joe Smith. Garnett paced Boston with 25 points in a losing effort. STUART CAHILL, BOSTON HERALD

Opposite: Celtics forward Glen Davis attempts to find daylight underneath Cleveland's Ben Wallace. STUART CAHILL, BOSTON HERALD

ANOTHER ROADBLOCK HAS C'S HEADED BACK HOME

> Mark Murphy, *Boston Herald*

May 17, 2008

Coach Doc Rivers keeps saying that nights like this are fine as long as the Celtics still have a chance to clinch at home.

And that's exactly where his team is this morning — backed into its second straight Game 7, with about as much playoff rhythm as a robot.

The Celts dropped Game 6 last night, 74-69 to Cleveland — which won despite shooting 32.9 percent from the floor — and now face an Eastern Conference semifinal series finale tomorrow at the Garden.

From a two-point night by Rajon Rondo to continued struggles by Ray Allen (nine points on 3-for-8 shooting) to Rivers' insistence on sticking with a struggling Glen Davis, the Celtics were again an offensive mess on the road. Save for 25 points from Kevin Garnett and 16 from Paul Pierce — the only two Celtics in double figures — the team was very much a reflection of its 39.7 shooting percentage.

Their 69 points were a season low (including playoffs) and second-lowest all time for the team in the playoffs. They also were an all-time playoff low by a Cavaliers opponent.

Left: Boston's James Posey fights for possession of a loose ball with Cleveland's LeBron James (left) and Ben Wallace (right).
STUART CAHILL, BOSTON HERALD

Opposite: Paul Pierce attempts to strip the ball from Cleveland's LeBron James on a drive to the basket. James finished the game with 32 points and 12 rebounds.
STUART CAHILL, BOSTON HERALD

And now, for the second straight playoff series, the Celts are faced with a Game 7. Even if they are 7-0 at home in the playoffs, they are also tempting fate.

"I feel very good about it, with the leadership we have with our veterans," said Kendrick Perkins, who then acknowledged that there's such a thing as pushing one's luck.

"Nobody wants to be in the position of playing a Game 7. But when you have homecourt in Boston, it makes a big difference."

It won't if the Celtics continue to break down.

Last night the problem was misses — lots of them, like an 0-for-15, four-turnover, two-point stretch that extended from late in the second quarter into the third, a total of 9:12.

To the Celtics' credit, they immediately came back from that 16-point deficit, got to within three in the third and as close as five in the fourth.

But this time, LeBron James scored 19 of his game-high 32 points in the second half.

And the Cavs, who led the league in offensive rebounding during the regular season, collected 16 last night for a 17-2 edge in second-chance points.

"It's just losing, period, that gets to you," James Posey said. "We could have done a better job of taking care of the ball and of getting stops. They didn't shoot well but they made plays. That was the big thing."

The Celtics wasted some solid first-half work last

night.

But just when they seemed to be down for the count, they struck back. Despite trailing by 13 points (65-52) with 9:55 left in the fourth, they suddenly clicked with an 8-0 run that included jumpers from Pierce and Garnett, the latter cutting the deficit to 65-60.

But James answered in a big way, first with a spinning drive and then with a 20-footer AFTER Pierce got a hand on the ball for a 69-60 Cavs lead with 4:08 left.

Eddie House followed with his second 3 of the night, but the Celtics failed to convert on the next possession when Garnett missed and then traveled after an offensive rebound.

With 2:10 left, Wally Szczerbiak then buried a 3 for a 72-63 Cleveland lead.

And yet the Celtics came back again, this time on a Kendrick Perkins dunk and two Pierce free throws. After two James misses, Allen was fouled on a fast break and hit both free throws to cut the C's deficit to 72-69. Seconds earlier Pierce was whistled for a charge on James — a call that had the Celtics bench up in arms.

After several timeouts, the Celtics sent Joe Smith to the line with 14.4 seconds left, and the veteran hit both free throws for a 74-69 lead. Pierce missed a heavily guarded 3-point attempt, James grabbed the rebound with four seconds to go and he fired the ball into the far end zone as the buzzer sounded.

BOSTON
MAY 18, 2008

CELTICS
97

CAVALIERS
92

Below: Celtics captain Paul Pierce celebrates a sweet Game 7 victory against Cleveland. Pierce's 41-point effort outshined a 45-point effort from Cleveland star LeBron James. MATTHEW WEST, BOSTON HERALD

Opposite: Kevin Garnett battles for a rebound with Cleveland's Ben Wallace. Garnett scratched out a double-double with 13 points and 13 rebounds. MATTHEW WEST, BOSTON HERALD

OH, CAPTAIN!

>Mark Murphy, *Boston Herald*

May 19, 2007

Late in the third quarter, after LeBron James hit an improbable shot to answer another of Paul Pierce's improbable shots, the two stars paused in front of the Celtics bench as the ball was inbounded.

Then they smiled at each other.

Game 7 of the Eastern Conference semifinals was burning hotter than Atlanta, but Pierce and James were somehow on speaking terms.

"We were, like, 'Who's going to give in?'" Pierce said. "It took six games for our offense to finally show up. But I think I said something about two years ago, when he had 50 and I had something like 40."

The score from that game is long forgotten. The Celtics' 97-92 win over Cleveland yesterday at the Garden, however, is being minted in franchise lore even as the C's prepare for tomorrow's conference finals opener against Detroit.

Pierce was right.

After six games of ugliness, a work of art exploded onto the canvas yesterday, courtesy of a shootout between Pierce and James that did justice to the legendary firefight between Larry Bird and Dominique Wilkins in Game 7 of the Eastern Conference semifinals in 1988.

Bird (34 points) and Wilkins (47) combined for 81 points in the C's 118-116 triumph that day. Pierce (41) and James (45) combined for 86 yesterday.

By the time the captain hit a free throw that bounced high off the back of the rim before dropping through for a 96-92 lead with 7.9 seconds left, everyone concerned knew a special game was about to end.

"I thought the ghost of Red (Auerbach) was looking over us," Pierce said. "You know, I wish he was here today to be with us, but I think that was him looking over us that guided the ball in. I think he kind of tapped it in the right direction, and it went through the net and it sort of put a smile on my face. Just the way the night was going."

Below: The Celtics get a round of applause from team owner Wyc Grousbeck (second from left), his wife, Corinne, and Red Sox owners John Henry (middle right) and Larry Lucchino (far right). MATT STONE, BOSTON HERALD.

Opposite: Paul Pierce dives for a loose ball during the fourth quarter of Game 7. Boston held off a fierce Cleveland rally to secure the victory. MATT STONE, BOSTON HERALD.

Just the way the playoffs are going, too.

The Celtics survived their second straight Game 7 despite a dominant performance from James. On the way to scoring 49 percent of Cleveland's points, he shot 14-of-29 from the field, 14-of-19 from the free throw line and 3-of-11 from 3-point range. He also led the Cavs with six assists.

But Pierce was just as driven, shooting 13-of-23 from the floor, 11-of-12 from the line and 4-of-6 from downtown. He had five assists.

The C's also received a pair of defining role performances. Eddie House provided energy and defense. And P.J. Brown pulled off a string of big plays down the stretch.

James scored eight straight Cleveland points before Brown tipped a Pierce miss out to Kevin Garnett, who hit a 10-foot turnaround for an 87-82 Celtics lead with 3:43 left.

The 38-year-old veteran then grabbed another offensive rebound and laid it in for an 89-84 edge.

The Cavs cut the margin to 89-88 with a 4-0 burst. But after a James miss, Brown grabbed the defensive board and buried an open 18-footer on the other end for a 91-88 lead.

Then, Pierce beat James in perhaps their most head-to-head confrontation.

James Posey rebounded Delonte West's missed trey but was tied up by Zydrunas Ilgauskas. The 7-foot-3 Lithuanian won the tip, but Pierce dove between James and the ball and held on long enough to call a timeout.

Ray Allen hit two free throws with 18.8 seconds left, James missed the first of two some two seconds later, and House drained a pair from the line to give the Celtics a 95-89 advantage with 16.3 seconds to go. Sasha Pavlovic buried an open 3 that cut the Cavs' margin to 95-92, but after he was fouled, Pierce watched his high bouncer off the back rim fall in.

With seconds remaining, James missed his third shot in the last 1:21, and Cleveland got the rebound. House, however, stole the ball, drove the floor and heaved it into the stands at the buzzer.

"Like Paul said, this is emotional," Garnett said. "We will enjoy this, but as we advance it will get a little more difficult."

After 14 contentious playoff games, though, the C's have a good frame of reference.

CELTICS
88
PISTONS
79

BOSTON
MAY 20, 2008

Left: Kevin Garnett, who scored 26 points on 11-for-17 shooting, celebrates after hitting a jump shot against the Pistons. MATTHEW WEST, BOSTON HERALD

Opposite: Ray Allen dangles from the rim after dunking the ball for two of his nine points. MATTHEW WEST, BOSTON HERALD

C'S CONTROL THE TAP

>Mark Murphy, *Boston Herald*

May 21, 2008

Maybe they really did need seven games against Cleveland to develop a tough outer shell. Maybe, after 15 playoff contests and two Game 7s, the Celtics last night finally were the toughened postseason product that many were starting to question.

The Celtics opened the Eastern Conference finals with an 88-79 win against Detroit that they were able to control with authority.

They might not want more than a day between games ever again.

"I've been saying it for a while, but I like this rhythm of every other day," coach Doc Rivers said. "I didn't want to go 14 games to get here, but I really think it's helped us.

"Later, if we get fatigued, then we'll be wrong."

He won't hear any complaints from the rank and file.

Kevin Garnett had one of his purest shooting performances (11-for-17) of the postseason, finishing with 26 points and raising his average in four games against Detroit this season to 24.7.

Paul Pierce followed up his 41-point effort in Game 7 against the Cavs with 22 last night despite being guarded by one of the toughest wing defenders in the league, Tayshaun Prince.

"Whenever you play so many games in the playoffs, you learn so much about yourselves," Pierce said. "We're the only team in the league that's played 14 games coming into this series, so we've learned a lot. And this team has learned to keep its composure, especially when the lead (has broken) down, and we know how to execute our plays."

Left: Rajon Rondo, who hit an open three-point shot to bury Detroit's comeback hopes, sprints past the Pistons' bench after giving the Celtics an 83-73 lead. MATTHEW WEST, BOSTON HERALD

Opposite: Celtics head coach Doc Rivers makes his point to his team during a timeout. STUART CAHILL, BOSTON HERALD

The Celtics have Rajon Rondo to thank for part of that composure. The young point guard, who had an up-and-down existence in the first two playoff series and in the three regular-season meeting with the Pistons, blitzed Detroit with 11 points, seven assists and five steals.

The Pistons, with a subpar Chauncey Billups attempting to develop a rhythm after a two-game layoff because of a sore hamstring, were more turnover-prone than usual.

Rondo jumped on the opportunity to pressure the ball, and the Celts had more fast-break opportunities than they saw in the entire Cleveland series.

In addition to making a concerted effort to go into the paint early with Garnett, the Celtics attacked with Rondo at the top of the circle.

The bonus arrived when he buried two huge open jumpers — a baseline 20-footer for an 83-73 lead with 2:42 left, and an unguarded 3-pointer with 1:47 left for an 86-75 edge.

Rondo has been tentative about taking these so-called dare shots when his confidence is low. Rivers can only hope last night's results finally drove the point home to Rondo that he has to make the other team pay for lax coverage.

"Yeah, but I've done that before," Rivers said. "I believe in him, I play him, and I'm going to keep playing him. Everything I told him before the game was, 'Stop worrying about them, and make them worry about you. You're a hell of a basketball player.'

"But for the last 48 hours I didn't hear anything about how Rondo could play. It was about everyone else."

That changed with 2:42 left. Detroit had come as close as six points before the Celtics started to pull away. Garnett kicked out to Rondo on the left baseline for the clutch 20-footer.

Hamilton was fouled on the next drive — with 2:10 left — and hit both to cut the margin to eight.

But Rondo, challenged to shoot throughout the conference semifinals by Cleveland, buried an open 3-pointer off a kick-out from Ray Allen to kill Detroit's hopes.

Billups missed the second of two free throws, and with 44 seconds left, Pierce hit from 12 feet.

The Celtics captain stole the ball and ran down the clock before missing a meaningless shot. The same could be said of Prince's game-ending trey.

BOSTON
MAY 22, 2008

PISTONS
103
CELTICS
97

Below: Glen Davis wrestles for the ball with Pistons guard Rodney Stuckey. MATT STONE, BOSTON HERALD

Opposite: Tony Allen leaps to attempt to block the shot of Pistons guard Richard Hamilton, who led Detroit scorers with 25 points. MATT STONE, BOSTON HERALD

AN IN-HOUSE PROBLEM

\>Mark Murphy, *Boston Herald*
May 23, 2008

The home cooking diet has been suspended. Now the Celtics HAVE to produce where they have run on empty during this postseason — the road.

Homecourt advantage — that precious commodity the Celtics managed to protect through their first two playoff series — was wiped off the board with a 103-97 loss to Detroit in Game 2 of the Eastern Conference finals last night at the Garden.

In becoming the first team to break serve on the C's, Detroit tied the series at 1 entering Game 3 at The Palace at Auburn Hills tomorrow night.

Kevin Garnett, facing up to the issue, gave an affirmative nod. Like his teammates, Garnett knew this challenge would arrive.

"There's going to come a time when we've got to get one, and we've finally come up front, you know, with that dilemma," he said. "We've got to find some way to win on the road, and that's what it is."

There also was one part the Celts didn't necessarily expect to resurface last night — defensive breakdowns.

They may have suffered through the occasional lapses — especially on the road — against Atlanta and

Left: Ray Allen, who finished with 25 points on 9-for-16 shooting, keeps the ball from Detroit guard Richard Hamilton. MATT STONE, BOSTON HERALD

Opposite: Celtics Kevin Garnett and Kendrick Perkins go up for the loose ball against Pistons Theo Ratliff and Antonio McDyess. STUART CAHILL, BOSTON HERALD

Cleveland. But last night's breakdown — the Pistons shot 49.3 percent from the field, including 52.4 percent in the fourth quarter — was disturbing.

Beyond impressive shooting in the second half from the likes of Detroit's Rodney Stuckey, Rasheed Wallace and Antonio McDyess, the Celtics also were slow to catch up with the ball.

Not even a second-half resurgence by the previously slumping Ray Allen (25 points, 9-for-16) or the fact that Paul Pierce (26 points) and Garnett (24) also shot the ball well was good enough.

Lingering questions about Chauncey Billups' health were answered. The Pistons point guard forgot about his sore hamstring and came across with a 19-point, seven-assist gem that gave Detroit all the direction it needed.

And though the Celtics outrebounded the Pistons 39-31, they gave up four back-breaking offensive boards in the fourth quarter.

"Down the stretch we scored out of every timeout, but they came out and scored out of every timeout, too," Celtics coach Doc Rivers said. "Their offensive rebounding was a killer. They made plays down the stretch, and we didn't make enough."

The Celtics continually ran into a nine-point barrier until P.J. Brown sandwiched two jumpers around an Allen dunk, cutting their deficit to five (86-81) with 6:22 remaining.

Garnett scored off a Pierce bullet pass, and Allen continued to heat up, answering a McDyess jumper with a trey from the top of the circle and then hitting a 10-footer off the dribble.

That basket cut the margin to two points (90-88) for the second time in 30 seconds, and Garnett soon made it a third (92-90) with a 15-footer.

The Pistons, however, responded by taking a 96-90 lead with 2:20 left when Wallace followed up a Tayshaun Prince 20-footer with a baseline jumper for the team's fifth score in six possessions.

Garnett cut the margin to four with his own 20-footer, but Allen missed from 10 feet out the next time down. Richard Hamilton drove in a nail with a floater for a 98-92 advantage with 48 seconds left. Pierce followed with a lefty drive, but, off an inbounds pass, Billups broke free of James Posey off a pick for a reverse layup and a 100-94 lead with 18.7 seconds to go. Allen hit a deep, guarded trey that cut the Detroit lead to 100-97 with 10.7 seconds left, but Wallace was fouled on the subsequent inbounds play and iced it by hitting the first of two free throws.

@ DETROIT MAY 24, 2008	
CELTICS	94
PISTONS	80

Below: Celtics head coach Doc Rivers welcomes Kevin Garnett to the bench. STUART CAHILL, BOSTON HERALD

Opposite: Kevin Garnett, who had a double-double with 22 points and 13 rebounds, goes up for a shot attempt while being fouled by Detroit forward Jason Maxiell. STUART CAHILL, BOSTON HERALD

CELTICS FINALLY START MOTORING IN DETROIT

>Mark Murphy, *Boston Herald*

May 25, 2008

All they needed was a little desperation, the panic of finally having someone pull the parquet out from under their feet.

The Celtics, in their 17th playoff game, finally won on the road, taking a 2-1 Eastern Conference finals lead with last night's 94-80 win over Detroit.

"Maybe somebody taking away our security blanket was what we needed," coach Doc Rivers said.

Paul Pierce had talked about carrying a gorilla on his back as the road losses piled up — the total reaching six

straight before last night. The Celtics hadn't won on the road since a regular-season game April 14 in New York.

But Pierce's gorilla finally was put back in the cage last night without a lot of fanfare.

"You know, the whole time throughout this, we didn't feel like we hadn't won a road game," he said. "Before the game I told the guys, 'Hey, during the regular season we were the best team on the road, so let's go out there and try to show them.'

"Everything that happened before is behind us — this

Left: Rajon Rondo is double teamed by Pistons defenders Chauncey Billups and Rasheed Wallace.
STUART CAHILL, BOSTON HERALD

Opposite: Richard Hamilton pushes Celtics guard Ray Allen out of bounds. Allen had a poor shooting night from the floor, finishing 5 for 16.
STUART CAHILL, BOSTON HERALD

starts right now, zero-zero. That's the way we came out from the start of the game."

Ultimately this win came together with a rare balance between the starters and the bench — the former with a great start, and the latter with some important contributions once Kevin Garnett and Ray Allen fell into quick foul trouble in the first quarter.

With both players on the bench, a unit that included the on-again Sam Cassell and P.J. Brown closed out the quarter with a 10-0 run for an early 25-17 lead that frustrated the Pistons the rest of the way.

Detroit, its only lead of the game (17-15) behind it, never got closer than four points the rest of the way.

With the exception of Garnett's 22-point, 13-rebound double-double, the stars on both sides took a back seat last night. Chauncey Billups (six points, four assists) spent one telling 11-minute stretch on the bench between the third and fourth quarters.

Pierce attempted only six shots, though he made the most of it with 11 points that included a pair of 3-point daggers in the third and fourth quarters. Allen, though active, had another rough night with 14 points on 5-of-16 shooting.

Instead, the game was taken over by role players like Kendrick Perkins, who supplied a furious inside game with 12 points and 10 rebounds on 6-of-7 shooting.

His interior play accentuated a 34-24 edge by the Celtics in points in the paint, as well as a 19-10 advantage in second-chance points and 44-28 in rebounds.

But that's how badly the Pistons, beyond another inspired night by Rodney Stuckey (17 points), struggled with the ball. They shot 38.4 percent for the game. And it all went back to their slow start.

"We've been that way in our three games against them," Detroit coach Flip Saunders said. "I thought we were almost hyperactive offensively, and then all of a sudden you don't react defensively and end up looking bad because of it."

Bad reactions aside, the Pistons still managed to chop a 24-point Celtics lead down to nine (87-78) with 2:56 left on a Tayshaun Prince dunk.

Perhaps jolted by the threat, the Celtics responded. Garnett rebounded a Pierce miss, drew the foul and hit a free throw with 2:17 left, then followed a miss by Stuckey and posted up to finish off a bank hook for a 90-78 lead with 1:09 left.

KEVIN GARNETT

KG takes on big responsibilities

›Tony Massarotti, Boston Herald
May 26, 2008

The NBA Finals are just two wins away now, and you cannot help but get the feeling Kevin Garnett finally has decided to take more of this upon himself. In the NBA, only championships can validate the greatest players. Maybe that is why Garnett now seems like a man on a mission.

"He's never played in the Finals. He understands it. You've got to do it now," said Celtics guard Sam Cassell, who knows Garnett as well as anyone currently connected with the team. "You've got to go after it while it's in sight."

Yes, the Finals are in sight now, though it really should come as no surprise; after all, it is much easier to see when you are on the shoulders of a man who is basically 7 feet tall. The 6-foot-11 Garnett is averaging precisely 24 points, 11.7 rebounds, 3.7 assists, 1.3 blocks and a steal in the first three games of the Eastern Conference finals. The Detroit Pistons have had such difficulty containing him that it is enough to make their coach flip.

On Saturday, in Game 3 of this series, Garnett finished with 22 points and 13 rebounds in what was easily the Celtics' most important win of the season. Of his six assists, three resulted in layups or dunks. Garnett is passing a little less and shooting a little more, and that is precisely what the Celtics need him to do at a time when elite players draw the fine line that ultimately will separate the most elite teams.

"I think he's been more determined in the post than he had been in the regular season," Celtics coach Doc Rivers said yesterday as the Celtics went through preparations for tonight's Game 4. "I thought during the regular season he would go away from it at times, almost on purpose, to get everybody else involved. But now when he gets it down low, he's looking to score and that's nice."

Dismissive of any attention that puts the individual before the team — Bill Belichick would love this man — Garnett currently is shrugging off his recent play as nothing more than him being "more aggressive." That humility is one of the great paradoxes of his personality. On the one hand, Garnett is a naturally intense competitor with the build and ferocity of a praying mantis; on the other, he is level-headed, rational, articulate and thoughtful.

What Garnett is, too, is indisputably real, the kind of rare superstar who scurries to pull up a fallen teammate (he does this all the time) and almost never calls attention to himself.

"Oh, he has an ego. You have to have an ego to be good in this league," Cassell mused. "Kev, he's a great teammate first and foremost. He's intense. He enjoys his teammates. But when it's time to play basketball, he becomes another person. His intensity level goes high."

Garnett has made it work lately, especially, going back to the Cleveland series. It was in a Game 4 loss at Cleveland that Garnett took just 13 shots, scoring 15 points, when the message truly seemed to get through to him. WE NEED YOU TO DO MORE. Garnett has since averaged 22.7 points a game to go along with 10.3 rebounds, and he has averaged 17.5 shots a game.

"I think it's more him," Rivers said when asked about the obvious change in Garnett's play. "We have talked about it, but it's always him."

Said Garnett: "Just aggressive, nothing more, nothing less than that. Every time I've got a one-on-one, try to take it. Other than that, trying to make plays for my teammates."

If only it were all that easy.

Sam Cassell says of Kevin Garnett: "I think he's a little crazy, myself. But he makes it work." MATT STONE, BOSTON HERALD

PISTONS	94
CELTICS	75

@ DETROIT MAY 26, 2008

Below: Kevin Garnett (left) talks over a game situation with teammate Sam Cassell during a timeout. STUART CAHILL, BOSTON HERALD

Opposite: Paul Pierce, who had 16 points, drives the lane against Pistons forward Antonio McDyess. STUART CAHILL, BOSTON HERALD

NO SHOT IN GAME 4

>Mark Murphy, *Boston Herald*

May 27, 2008

The evening was painfully slow, marred by whistles and a lot of physical play.

The Celtics shot 31.8 percent from the field, hunted for baskets as if they were rare pearls and scored almost half of their points from the free throw line.

The offensive drought had a predictable effect — a 94-75 Game 4 loss to the Detroit Pistons that evened the Eastern Conference finals at 2 and again showed that the Celtics can look horrid with the ball in their hands.

"We talked about (offensive problems) at halftime, and then in the first four plays (of the third quarter) we came out and did the exact thing we talked about that we shouldn't do," coach Doc Rivers said. "We took the extra dribble and then made the pass instead of just making the pass. But give Detroit credit. I thought they bumped us off spots, were more physical and were more aggressive all night.

"Usually, the win goes to the team that was more aggressive, and it was them."

The brutish pace enabled the Celts to hang close — at least until Detroit broke away with a 16-2 run in the last 3:23.

And the biggest shot of the game-clinching spurt came from the one player who has struggled the most in this series. Chauncey Billups buried Detroit's first 3-pointer of the game to give the home team an 83-73 lead with 2:55 left.

The Celtics had gone 16:28 without a turnover before Ray Allen threw away the ball, leading to Billups' bomb.

Still, that was a much better run than they had in the first half. The C's finished the opening quarter with one assist compared to five turnovers. They had 11 turnovers and six assists by halftime.

Left: Kendrick Perkins pulls down a rebound against Detroit forward Rasheed Wallace.
STUART CAHILL, BOSTON HERALD

Opposite: Paul Pierce loses his dribble against Detroit forward Rasheed Wallace. Pierce had four turnovers in the game.
STUART CAHILL, BOSTON HERALD

"We just made it tougher on ourselves," Allen said. "We started off offensively on a bad note. . . . I think we only had one assist going into the second quarter, and anytime that happens, we're not going to do ourselves any favors trying to score.

"I think we've learned our lesson in the past — each individual trying to do it for themselves."

Indeed, a premium wasn't placed on passing.

The C's finished with only 12 assists — normally half of what they record in a game — including another low-ebb game from Rajon Rondo, who had four points and four assists. His backup, Sam Cassell, had zero points and zero assists in 16 minutes.

Still, the Celtics, who scored 32 points from the free throw line, cut their deficit to five points five separate times but could never get closer.

Garnett, limited to the perimeter all night, finally wheeled in with a baseline jump hook, but the Pistons, after losing out on many calls, got to the line when Richard Hamilton hit two free throws.

Allen uncharacteristically missed two free throws, and Hamilton put together a pair of insurance hoops — a drive and a 15-footer sandwiched around a Garnett miss that stretched the lead to 88-75.

"It's always disappointing," Allen said. "We pride ourselves on making our teammates better and allowing them to make us better. There's a point when you have to make the simple play. You cover a little space and then make the pass out, and you can live with that all night."

The Big Three of Pierce (16 points), Garnett (16) and Allen (11) combined for just 43 points.

Antonio McDyess had a game-high 21 points and 16 rebounds for Detroit.

BOSTON
MAY 28, 2008

CELTICS
106

PISTONS
102

Left: Kevin Garnett is congratulated by James Posey after hitting his first foul shot, which iced Boston's 106-102 victory in Game 5. MATTHEW WEST, BOSTON HERALD

Opposite: Kendrick Perkins scored 18 points and grabbed 16 rebounds in a stellar Game 5 performance. MATT STONE, BOSTON HERALD

CELTICS SECURE 3-2 LEAD IN SERIES

> Mark Murphy, *Boston Herald*

May 29, 2008

This was a night of transformation.

Kendrick Perkins morphed into Karl Malone. Kevin Garnett banked a 3-pointer — only his second of the season — and flexed his wrist like Reggie Miller. Chauncey Billups looked like his old self.

And Ray Allen, freed from the prison that has incarcerated his jumper for 18 playoff games, was Ray Allen again.

The Celtics guard exploded last night for 29 points, including a 21-point second half, at the most opportune time — a 106-102 win over Detroit in Game 5 of the Eastern Conference finals, with Game 6 set for tomorrow at the Palace.

Doc Rivers knew it was just a matter of time before his prized shooting guard rediscovered his stroke. But the Celtics coach sounds like he had simply stopped wondering when the cloud would finally burst.

"You just know he's a good player, and you don't stop believing that," Rivers said. "This has been a tough stretch for Ray, and I give him a ton of credit. No. 1, I thought this was his best defensive game of the series, and No. 2, throughout this he has never changed his routine."

Even with a monstrous 18-point, 16-rebound performance from Perkins, and a 33-point effort from Garnett that featured even more deep jumpers than usual, Allen's belief in himself may have ultimately been the difference last night.

It was that close, with Billups (26 points), Richard Hamilton (25) and Rasheed Wallace (6-of-9 from 3-point range) cutting the margin to a point (102-101) with 8.2 seconds left before the Celtics made their final game-clinching plays.

Though he shot 5-of-6 from downtown, no points were more important than Allen's two free throws with 6.3 seconds left, followed by two more from Garnett with 3.4 left.

Stuckey, intentionally put on the line twice in the last 8.2 seconds with the Celtics clinging to a three-point edge

Below: Kevin Garnett and Kendrick Perkins embrace after Boston's win, which brought the team one step closer to an NBA Finals appearance. MATT STONE, BOSTON HERALD

Opposite: Ray Allen, who helped seal the win by hitting two free throws with 6.3 seconds left, drives to the net for a bucket. MATTHEW WEST, BOSTON HERALD

each time, missed the first of two with 4.5 seconds left, leaving a little extra room for Garnett on his final trip to the line.

The missed free throw was crushing for Stuckey, who scored Detroit's last eight points, including a corner trey with 1:23 left that cut the deficit to 100-99.

As excruciating as the sequence was, it was also one of their most self-affirming moments of the postseason.

The Celtics, who have played more games (19) than any team still alive, have secured Game 5 in three straight playoff series, with the pivotal game coming at the Garden each time.

"We don't get this game, we put ourselves in the position to have to win another road game," Paul Pierce said. "We know how tough it is to win out there in Detroit. It's one of the biggest games that we played all year long. It was a crucial game at home. We had to get the lead just to get some momentum back, and we knew it was going to be one of the toughest games of the series. We said

coming in that this was going to be like a Game 7, and we responded. We knew it wasn't going to be easy."

Nowhere was that as evident as when the Pistons, with a 10-1 run, cut the C's lead to 92-88 with 4:46 left on a Billups 3.

The Celtics fought to maintain their edge, but slipped further when Rajon Rondo and Pierce each missed a free throw in the 38 seconds leading up to Stuckey's trey that pulled the Pistons within a point for the first time in the half. Allen had trouble feeding Garnett on the next possession, with the ball deflecting out off Hamilton with six seconds on the shot clock. Allen got the ball back on the left baseline and buried the jumper for a 102-99 lead as if he hadn't missed in a month.

The Pistons rebounded Billups' off-balance drive, called a timeout, and this time Billups put his drive off the front of the rim. The Celtics ran the clock down, and sweated out the last 10 seconds from the line.

@ DETROIT
MAY 30, 2008

CELTICS
89

PISTONS
81

Left: Kevin Garnett and guard Eddie House pump each other up before taking on the Detroit Pistons in Game 6. MATT STONE, BOSTON HERALD

Opposite: Rajon Rondo slices through the Pistons defense for two of his 11 points. MATT STONE, BOSTON HERALD

BRING ON THE LAKERS

>Mark Murphy, *Boston Herald*

May 31, 2008

They played 20 playoff games to reach this point, many of them grueling and unsightly.

But after suffering through two seven-game playoff series, and the pressure of a rested Lakers team awaiting them, the Celtics finally cut themselves a break last night.

They clinched a trip to the NBA's ultimate stage for the first time since 1987 with an 89-81 win over Detroit in Game 6 of the Eastern Conference finals.

Just like back then, they'll play the Lakers — a retro matchup that has been in the prayers of every league and television executive since director of basketball operations Danny Ainge stunned the league with trades for Kevin Garnett and Ray Allen last summer.

And until last night, it was also an old, dusty rivalry that few dared acknowledge.

"Somebody asked me in the beginning of the year what it was like to be part of it, and I said, 'Well, we hadn't really been a part of it yet,'" Allen said. "That's because we hadn't created our own rivalry, and it would take us

playing in the Finals.

"And here we are."

As well-conditioned as a team could be, to hear Flip Saunders tell it.

"I told Doc that they played well," the Pistons coach said. "It's tough as a team to go through the season as they did and the grind they have as the No. 1 seed (in the playoffs), to be where they're at when everyone is shooting for them. So that's a credit to what he's been able to do and what they've been able to do."

And yet there were many who questioned the Celtics' ability to close out games as well as series after they needed seven games to finish off the Hawks and Cavaliers in the first two rounds, respectively.

That specter appeared to loom last night in the midst of a physical, close-quarters struggle.

But Garnett and Paul Pierce took care of business down the stretch, the latter with 10 of his team-high 27 points in the fourth quarter, and the former with six vital points in the

Below: Paul Pierce celebrates after winning the Eastern Conference title. MATT STONE, BOSTON HERALD

Opposite: Paul Pierce scored 10 of his team-high 27 points in the fourth quarter. MATT STONE, BOSTON HERALD

first six minutes of the period after shooting 4-of-13 from the floor through the first three quarters.

Richard Hamilton shook off the pain of a strained right elbow to score 21 points for Detroit. Chauncey Billups, with a game-high 29, came through with his second straight gem.

But these were punches that the Celtics, after their long grind, were able to withstand.

After trailing by 10 points (70-60) early in the fourth, the Celts fired back with a 10-0 run to tie the score at 70 on a Pierce free throw. Garnett had scored four points in the run and came back with a 20-footer sandwiched between a pair of Jason Maxiell hoops.

Pierce then gave the Celtics the lead for good at 75-74 with a spinning drive and foul that he converted for a three-point play.

Defending that cushion, like their entire season, required a fight. Garnett hit a turnaround from the lane, a struggling Rasheed Wallace (2-for-12) missed, and Rajon Rondo buried the evening's biggest hoop — a 20-footer

from the right side.

The Celtics led by seven (83-76) when Billups converted a three-point play off a flat-lined leaner. James Posey stole the ball at midcourt, and Pierce hit two more free throws with 1:35 left for an 85-79 lead.

Yet, still the Celts didn't make it easy on themselves. Garnett missed two free throws with 36 seconds remaining and a six-point lead in hand.

But as Wallace and Hamilton missed jumpers, Pierce (1-for-2) and Ray Allen (2-for-2) salted the Eastern Conference title away at the stripe.

They had, yet again, taken someone's best shot.

"It's been tough," Allen said. "I think there have been points during the season where somebody has won a big game for us. We've been at points where we had to win games in the defensive end and some where we had to win them in the offensive end. We've faced so many obstacles.

"But we found out that we had character — that's the whole point. We definitely got better throughout the year."

2007/2008
NBA FINALS

PAUL PIERCE

Pierce heard Doc's call

›Mark Murphy, *Boston Herald*

June 3, 2008

There was a time, a little more than four years ago, when Doc Rivers would take Paul Pierce out of a game, and the Celtics captain would return to the bench looking straight ahead, anywhere but at his coach.

There was cold steam, generated by Pierce's famous stubbornness. The team didn't have much promise, and Pierce clearly wasn't buying into his new coach's plan.

Pierce freely talked about that old impasse yesterday. He and Rivers (as a coach) are about to make their first NBA Finals appearance together, and there's a good chance that one wouldn't be in this position without the other.

"Me and Doc definitely bumped heads in the beginning, and that makes it more important today," Pierce said after yesterday's practice. "Now? I love the guy."

Back then, the relationship was tumultuous.

"There were a couple of screaming matches. It was my rebelliousness coming out," Pierce said. "I just didn't think it would work out."

Rivers' refusal to back down, as well as a firm belief in his own system, eventually forced Pierce to take a long, hard look at himself.

The person staring back was ready to change.

"It was just about me maturing, after not believing," he said. "I had to go home for the summer and grow up. I had to stop pouting, and come back and help these young guys out. I had to tell myself, 'You're still the captain of this team, so go out and play like it.'"

At this time last year, Pierce and Kobe Bryant were working out together at UCLA. The Lakers star had just told ESPN that he wanted a trade, and after talking with Pierce, they decided to make a bet.

Pierce won't reveal the terms, perhaps in part because neither player had to pay up. They both stayed home. No one knows the odds, but both ended up, with some significant help, leading their teams to the NBA Finals.

For Pierce, it's the ultimate proof of finally putting his trust in Rivers. The coach noted early in the process that for all of Pierce's reluctance, his numbers had also improved. And those numbers, especially in terms of field goal percentage, continued to rise.

But Rivers wasn't worried about a little friction. It was a small price to pay for this year's ride.

"I expected it," he said of butting heads with Pierce when he first came aboard. "I knew what the right thing was for him and the team. I knew it would happen, but give him all the credit for how he finally responded to it."

Pierce isn't being glib when he says he "loves the guy."

He's playing his boyhood team, the Lakers, in the Finals. He no longer heads a locker room of novices, but he appreciates where that experience has brought him.

"My final thought was, 'You're still the captain of this team, so go out and play like it,'" he said. "... What we have now is a combination of us and Doc," he said. "We talk about all of these things. The ultimate goal is to win ballgames. Who cares who scores if we're all winners? We've all got accolades, but we haven't won a championship. You look at Kevin (Garnett) and Ray (Allen), and at the end of the day you always see them as unselfish ballplayers.

"It was the way I knew I COULD play. A lot of people didn't think I could make the adjustment."

But the most important believer, beyond Pierce, was his coach.

Paul Pierce and Boston head coach Doc Rivers embrace after punching their ticket to the NBA Finals. MATT STONE, BOSTON HERALD

THE TEAM

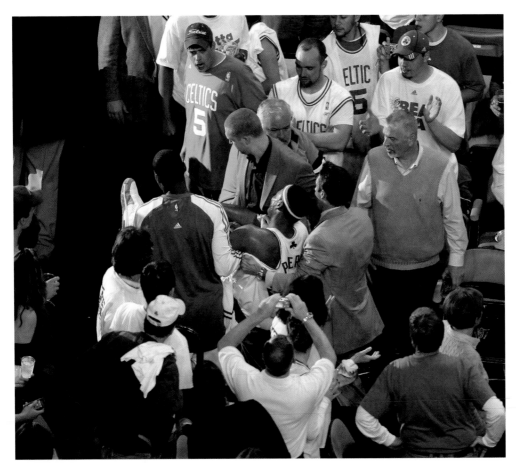

Left: Tony Allen and Brian Scalabrine help team physician Brian McKeon carry Paul Pierce off the court after he was injured in the third quarter against the Lakers. MATTHEW WEST, BOSTON HERALD

Opposite: Ray Allen, who hit several clutch three-point shots in the last quarter, looks to pass the ball. MATT STONE, BOSTON HERALD

CAPTAIN COMES OFF FLOOR

>Mark Murphy, *Boston Herald*

June 6, 2008

It's the kind of story that will grow entirely out of proportion in the re-telling. In another 20 years, perhaps Paul Pierce will be remembered for shrugging off the effects of a broken leg to return and lead the Celtics to a Game 1 win over the Lakers.

In truth it was a strained right knee that required Pierce to be carried off the floor. The captain's return from that third quarter injury provided all the energy and emotion the Celtics needed in their 98-88 win over the Lakers last night for a 1-0 series lead in the NBA Finals.

"One thing we know about P is that he's very tough, and we've seen him play through numerous injuries throughout the season," said fellow forward Kevin Garnett. "There were times when we thought he wasn't going to play, and

he played. He played his best, if you ask me. And when he came (back) out, you just heard the roar of the crowd. He was walking, he was up on his own strength, and he rejuvenated us.

"I think it was to the point where he gave everybody life."

Pierce finished with 22 points, didn't limp once, and Garnett, after missing his nine previous shots, punctuated the night with a monstrous tip dunk that had a cowing effect on the Lakers.

Though Kobe Bryant scored 24 points, he needed 26 shots to get there. And Pau Gasol had 15 points, only three in the second half, when the Celtics finally took control.

The Lakers played the second half on the Celtics'

Left: Boston fans applaud as Paul Pierce returns to the court following an injury to his knee. MATTHEW WEST, BOSTON HERALD

Opposite: P.J. Brown celebrates with Paul Pierce following Pierce's return to the game. MATT STONE, BOSTON HERALD

terms. Though they shot 50 percent in the first half, a number that had coach Doc Rivers railing at halftime, they finished at 41.6 percent. That, in turn, resulted from a 42.1 percent third quarter and a 25 percent (5-of-20) fourth.

Pierce may have returned to hero worship from the crowd, but it was actually the Celtics defense, once again, that made the result possible.

Bryant, who hit one of his first seven shots, also hit only one of his last seven in the loss.

"I just missed some really, really good looks," he said. "I'll be thinking about those a little bit tonight."

The Celtics, on the other hand, may want to concentrate on what went right in the second half.

The crowd went quiet when, with 6:49 left in the third quarter, Pierce crashed to the floor during a Bryant drive and cried out in pain. After curling up and holding his right knee, he was carried off the floor by Tony Allen, Brian Scalabrine and team physician Brian McKeon. Once in the hallway, they put Pierce in a wheelchair and rolled him into the locker room.

But 5:04 was left when Pierce came running back into the arena to a roaring reception with a brace on his right knee. He ran past Rivers and immediately checked back in, with the Garden sound system playing the "Rocky"

theme song as Ray Allen hit two free throws for a 64-62 Celtics lead.

Pierce hit a free throw 23 seconds later, and the Celtics continued to feed off the crowd, which in turn continued to feed off Pierce's return.

Even as Bryant was elevating with a 12-point quarter, Pierce continued to drive the crowd. He hit a deep pullup trey off the break with 1:25 left for a 72-71 lead, and the next time down took a transition kick-out from Ray Allen and buried another 3-pointer for a 75-71 edge. Then, with the Celtics holding a 77-73 lead at the start of the fourth, he returned to the locker room for treatment.

By the time he came out early in the fourth, the Celts were about to put together two murderous hoops — a Sam Cassell jumper after Garnett leaped into the backcourt to tip a potential backcourt violation to P.J. Brown, who fed Cassell, and an open trey from James Posey for an 86-78 lead with 8:44 left.

The Lakers cut that score to 90-84 on an Lamar Odom three-point play with 2:51 left, but Allen gave the Celtics a major boost when he up-faked Sasha Vujacic, drew the foul and hit the second of two for a 91-85 Celtics lead.

Gasol hit one of two 40 seconds later, but the Celts were now in solid position for a battle of free throws and were able to close out Game 1 from there.

BOSTON
JUNE 8, 2008

CELTICS
108

LAKERS
102

Left: Leon Powe, who had a 21-point, five-dunk performance, slam dunks over Lakers center Ronny Turiaf.
MATT STONE, BOSTON HERALD

Opposite: Eddie House (left) and Sam Cassell celebrate as the Celtics take a 2-0 series lead against the Lakers.
STUART CAHILL, BOSTON HERALD

C'S HOLD POWE-SITION

›Mark Murphy, *Boston Herald*

June 9, 2008

The Celtics, on the verge of pulling off a rare playoff blowout, behaved like careless front-runners last night.

In the NBA Finals, there is no such thing as an airtight 24-point lead, which is what they had with 7:55 remaining.

When Kobe Bryant is on the floor, no one gets to go home early, though the Celtics apparently thought they were in line for a slide.

But even with that lapse, the C's emerged with something precious as the result of their whittled-down 108-102 win over the Lakers at the Garden — a 2-0 lead in the best-of-seven series.

After all, the result, and not the means, still is the point.

"Well, I was a little disappointed in our play the last six minutes of the game," C's captain Paul Pierce said. "I thought we just weren't aggressive enough to put the game away.

"We played like we just wanted the time to run out, and we were — myself, I was a little lackadaisical with the ball.

It's a great win but definitely a lesson to be learned in the last six minutes. Down the stretch, we've just got to be more aggressive. We're happy that we won, but at the same time, we definitely learned a valuable lesson there in the fourth quarter."

Pierce, who sprained his right knee in Game 1 on Thursday, played 41 minutes last night, finished with 28 points, was 4-for-4 on 3-point attempts and added eight assists.

But this was far from a one-man effort.

The Celtics threw the entire arsenal at the Lakers, including a 21-point, five-dunk performance from reserve Leon Powe and a 16-assist gem from energized point guard Rajon Rondo, who had as many assists (12) as the entire Lakers team at halftime.

Kobe Bryant once again had to work far too hard for his points.

He poured in a game-high 30 on 23 shots, though the

Lakers star may have discovered his form with a furious 13-point performance in the final 7:38 that nearly tipped this one into the Pacific.

"I thought we got cute when we got the lead," said Celtics coach Doc Rivers, whose team now hits the road for Game 3 tomorrow night at Staples Center.

"We started trying to make sensational plays instead of trying to make it simple, and when you play a team like that, that has that arsenal, they made shots. But we allowed them to get comfortable."

Amazingly enough, the Lakers cut back into this one despite a result that had many in the LA locker room — as well as up on the postgame podium — bemoaning the Celtics' 38-10 edge in free throw attempts.

Of particular agitation for coach Phil Jackson was the fact that Powe, 9-for-13 from the line in just 14 minutes, attempted more free throws than the entire Lakers team.

"I've never seen a game like that in all these years I've coached in the Finals. Unbelievable," Jackson said.

The Celtics had a 102-86 advantage, courtesy of a James Posey 3-pointer with 3:38 left, when they fell asleep at the switch.

A putback from Vladimir Radmanovic and treys from Bryant and Sasha Vujacic cut the Celts' lead to four.

Bryant then hit two free throws to make it 104-102 with 38.4 seconds left before Pierce got fouled on a drive and hit both for a 106-102 advantage with 22.8 seconds to go.

Vujacic, who already had two treys in the quarter, lined up for a third, but Pierce blocked it. Posey grabbed the rebound, drew the foul and hit both free throws.

Derek Fisher badly missed a trey, the Celtics got the rebound and could finally exhale.

"We (weren't) happy with how we ended the game," Garnett said. "Obviously we've got to be a lot more aggressive in the fourth quarter. We didn't do some of the same things that got us the lead, and it's a live-and-learn kind of thing."

LAKERS
87
....
CELTICS
81

Left: Paul Pierce (left) and Rajon Rondo look on from the bench during Game 3. STUART CAHILL, BOSTON HERALD

Opposite: Paul Pierce slams the ball in frustration. Pierce struggled during Game 3, scoring just six points on 2-for-14 shooting. MATT STONE, BOSTON HERALD

PIERCE, CELTICS OFF MARK

>Mark Murphy, *Boston Herald*

June 11, 2008

Inglewood wasn't proud last night.

Those in Paul Pierce's old neighborhood who traded in purple jerseys for green may be demanding a reverse swap this morning.

The Celtics captain, in his much-anticipated homecoming — with a 27-point career average at Staples Center and the Forum — had a night that will stain the legacy.

Above all, the Celtics followed his six-point, 2-for-14 lead in their 87-81 loss to the Lakers, cutting their edge in the NBA Finals to 2-1.

Pierce and another suffering Celtic — the 6-for-21 Kevin Garnett — shot a combined 8-for-35 in the face of an oddity.

The Lakers, the most high-powered offense of the postseason, actually won a game while scoring fewer than 90 points.

They are 10-22 in that category, winning last night in part thanks to a 34-22 edge in free throw attempts that some might ascribe to Phil Jackson's prolonged lament about the Celtics' Game 2 edge at the line.

But Doc Rivers told his players not to think, even for a second, Jackson's politicking had anything to do with what went wrong.

Kobe Bryant scored 11 of his 36 points from the line. Pau Gasol made two big plays off the offensive glass down the stretch, Sasha Vujacic (20 points) came off the bench with two huge fourth quarter treys, and the C's fell back on their heels.

"That team attacked — they were the aggressor," Rivers said. "That's why they went to the foul line, and they deserved it.

"The good part of the game is that our defense was pretty good, not great. Our offense was not. When Paul

Left: Kobe Bryant, who had 36 points, shoots over Celtics forward Leon Powe. STUART CAHILL, BOSTON HERALD

Opposite: Kendrick Perkins emphatically dunks the ball for two of his eight points. STUART CAHILL, BOSTON HERALD

has a night like this and Kevin has a night like this, and it was two or four points all game, I looked at it that we had a chance to steal the game when our guys were off."

Pierce wasn't even willing to go that far.

"We just lost the game — you can't make any more of it than that," he said. "There are no moral victories. But we can't expect them to go out and play the way they did tonight. Just stay positive and come back.

"But I thought we settled. We didn't put pressure on them to defend."

The Celtics were forced to go for most of the second half without Rajon Rondo, who suffered a strained ankle early in the third quarter. Though replacement Eddie House supplied a wealth of energy as well as two 3-pointers, and Ray Allen had one of his finest shooting performances of the playoffs with 25 points (8-for-13 from the floor), the shortcomings of Garnett and Pierce were too much to overcome.

Rondo was left on the bench down the stretch in favor of House not because of his injury, according to Rivers,

but House's effectiveness. Such was the state of the Celtics lineup over the last five minutes.

Two straight put-backs by Gasol gave the Lakers a 77-70 lead with 4:18 left. Pierce was fouled on a drive but failed to convert the three-point play, and Gasol hit the second of two free throws for a 78-72 edge.

Two Pierce free throws trimmed the margin to four, and Garnett spun into the lane with his most overpowering hoop of the night.

But Vujacic, a pain in the C's perimeter all night, buried an open corner trey for an 81-76 lead with 1:53 left, and after a blown layup from Garnett, Derek Fisher hit two free throws for a seven-point edge (83-76) with 1:33 left.

Garnett broke loose for an open dunk four seconds later, and House hit a 3-pointer to answer a Bryant jumper, but the Celtics were running out of clock.

Bryant hit a 10-footer for an 87-81 lead with 38 seconds left. Garnett then committed an offensive foul and the Celtics had wasted their last solid chance.

CELTICS
97

LAKERS
91

@ LOS ANGELES
JUNE 12, 2008

Below: Paul Pierce, who had 20 points and contained Kobe Bryant, is flanked by Glen Davis (left) and P.J. Brown after Game 4 of the NBA Finals. MATT STONE, BOSTON HERALD

Opposite: Kevin Garnett pulls down one of his 11 rebounds in Game 4. MATT STONE, BOSTON HERALD

GOTTA 'C' IT TO BELIEVE IT

>Mark Murphy, *Boston Herald*

June 13, 2008

They trailed by 24 points in the second quarter. They had one assist at the end of the first. They were being measured for a Hollywood burial.

But this is, after all, the land of unbelievable scripts.

So here's another: The Celtics, after opening up in a flatlined state, climbed out of that hole to take a 3-1 NBA Finals lead over the Lakers with last night's improbable 97-91 win at Staples Center.

It was the largest comeback in the Finals since 1971, according to the Elias Sports Bureau. The previous high had been Houston's 20-point rally against Orlando in 1995.

For all that will be said of Paul Pierce (who had 20 points and perhaps the defensive job of his career on Kobe Bryant) and Ray Allen (who polished this one off with a game-breaking drive on Sasha Vujacic with 16 seconds left), it was the bench that turned in one of its finest nights of the year.

James Posey's 18-point performance included two fourth-quarter 3-pointers, and Eddie House, again chosen to play ahead of an ineffective Rajon Rondo, added 11 points, four rebounds and a lot of energy.

As pumped up as they were by the surge, the Celtics remained smart enough to stay on message with just one win to go for their 17th NBA title, and first since 1986.

"Yeah, I can taste it," said Kevin Garnett, who finished with 16 points and 11 rebounds despite a foul-plagued start. "But we know that we still have to have the focus, and it's no more than that. Like we did tonight, we have to understand that there are three quarters left to play. That's what we have going for us."

Bryant looked at it another way.

"We just wet the bed — a nice big one, too," he said. "One of those you have to put a towel over."

Until the Lakers re-emerge from their practice facility for Game 5 on Sunday, they will be left to wonder just how

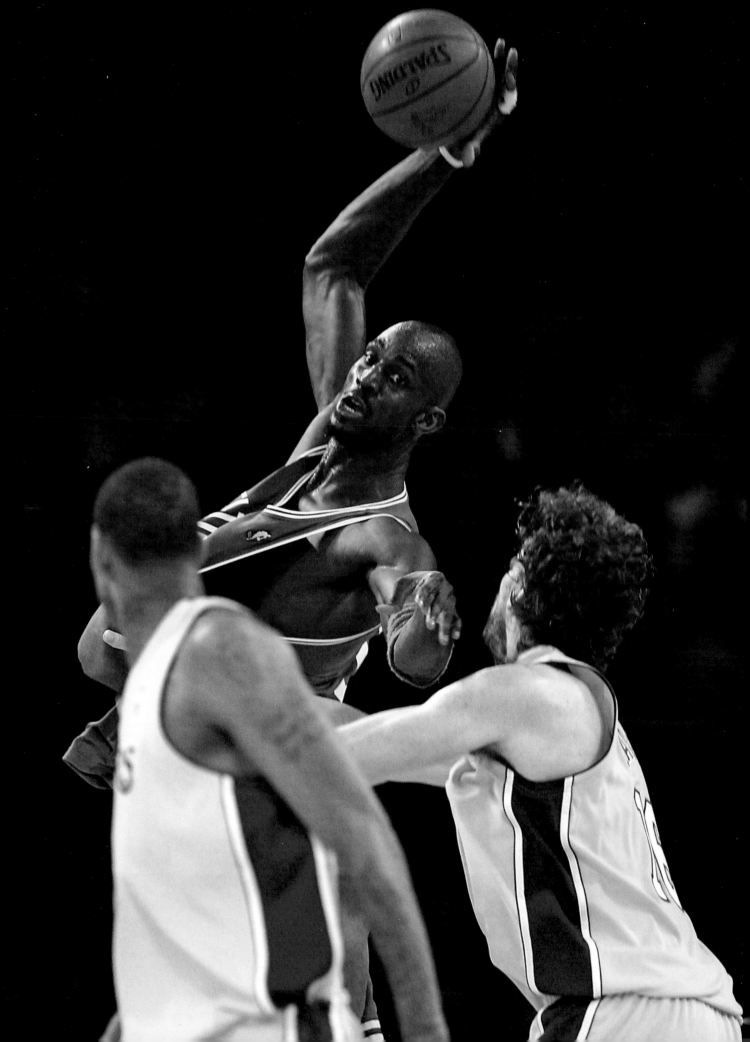

the Celtics escaped such a hole.

For even with their self-belief, the C's needed a spark.

Pierce provided it by asking to guard Bryant in the second half. The Lakers guard again worked too hard (6-for-19 from the field) for his points (17).

"I saw three or four bodies all night — as far as my personal rhythm it's a little harder to get going when that happens," Bryant said.

The Celtics, with Doc Rivers providing the halftime speech, had a different take.

"What was said was, 'Hang in there, No. 1. No. 2, that all the plays (in the first half) were made by them, all the hard plays,' " the coach said. "We had cut it to 11 once or to 13 once (in the first half), and every time we cut it they made a play.

"There was a loose ball that we didn't get that they saved. It led to a Luke Walton 3. It had nothing to do with X's and O's at that point. They made all the plays, and we didn't. So we could not win the game unless we defended and made plays. In the second half we made the plays."

The Celtics responded with a 31-point third quarter, powered by 61 percent shooting and defense that forced 27.8 percent Lakers efficiency.

It changed everything.

The Celtics had control with 1:30 left in the game when Bryant spun past Pierce and Garnett, cutting their lead to 89-87. Posey, however, buried his fourth trey of the night from the left corner for a 92-87 advantage with 1:13 to go.

Derek Fisher answered with a 20-footer nine seconds later, but Pierce shot back with two free throws. Pau Gasol then was given an easy dunk before Allen supplied the finishing touch.

The Celtics guard, isolated at the top of the circle on Vujacic, let the clock run down before driving past his man and converting for a 96-91 lead with 16 seconds remaining.

The Lakers got two chances on their last possession — misses by Vujacic and Bryant — before the Celtics ran out the clock.

RAY ALLEN

Allen plays a 'huge' role

》Tony Massarotti, Boston Herald

June 14, 2008

ay Allen waved off Kevin Garnett and squared up to the basket, and from that point on, Sasha Vujacic was pretty much toast. Allen juked. Vujacic buckled. And the Celtics had another signature moment, a piece of hardwood history all but narrated by James Earl Jones.

THIS GAME, THAT DRIVE, IT'S A PART OF OUR PAST, RAY. IT REMINDS OF EVERYTHING THAT ONCE WAS GOOD. AND THAT COULD BE AGAIN.

The Celtics are now just one win from their 17th NBA title and a funny thing has happened on the road back to redemption: As of today, old Mr. Allen is the Finals MVP. The Celtics still have a game to win and, perhaps, multiple games to play, but in the big picture that has been this extraordinary Celtics reversal, there has been no greater turnaround than the one belonging to Allen.

"Oh, it was huge. It was huge," coach Doc Rivers said of Allen's drive-and-deliver that all but finalized a 97-91 victory Thursday night over the Los Angeles Lakers in Game 4. "Paul (Pierce) was exhausted, and you could see it. I mean, he didn't even — on that play, he didn't want to come to the ball. It was really supposed to be a middle pick-and-roll with Kevin and Ray.

"Ray waved Kevin off because he liked the matchup that he had already, so he didn't want to bring another defender in to help. It was a great call by Ray. And then him getting to the basket was huge. The layup was just tremendous."

Vujacic? He looked more like Sasha Cohen, as if he was trying to defend Allen on ice skates. It's a miracle he didn't break one of his ankles.

Ah yes, the ankles. Remember them? The ankles were the reason many scoffed at the Allen acquisition last June,

when Celtics vice president of basketball operations Danny Ainge put what would become his master plan into motion. Allen was coming off double ankle surgery. He was about to turn 32. Allen did not have much left, many argued, and the Celtics were foolish to trade a package that included the No. 5 pick and Delonte West for a guy on borrowed time.

Allen heard all of that, to be sure, and anyone who bothered to listen closely enough got a glimpse of his competitiveness, too. During the Eastern Conference finals, when he was repeatedly asked about chasing around Rip Hamilton, Allen consistently dismissed the notion that he was tired. Every time someone asked what it was like to guard a man who was in such phenomenal physical condition, Allen tactfully delivered his reply.

I LIKE TO THINK I'M IN PRETTY GOOD SHAPE, TOO.

Now, 106 games into this Celtics season, Allen is coming off an outing in which he went the Full Monty, an Iversonian Game 4 effort in which he played the entire 48 minutes. In the Finals, Allen is averaging 43.5 minutes a game, more than any player on either team, including the otherworldly Kobe Bryant (42.8). He looks faster and quicker than most anyone else on the court, and his legs look none the worse for wear.

Old dog, new tricks.

"There was a point out there in the game where I knew I wasn't coming out, and I just said I have to suck it up," Allen said of his Game 4 performance. "I have plenty of time to rest the next couple of months, so suck it up."

Funny, isn't it? Relatively early in the Detroit series, when Allen was struggling badly, Rivers made the decision to keep Allen on the bench during some pivotal moments of the series. Now, the coach can't bring it upon himself to take the old man off the floor. In his last six games, Allen is 40-of-75 from the field (53.3 percent) and 20-of-39 from 3-point distance (51.3) while averaging a team-leading 21 points per game. He has even grabbed 5.6 rebounds a contest, including nine in Game 4 against the Lakers.

Maybe, in retrospect, what we have here is not an old Ray Allen but, rather, the Ray Allen of old.

Neither Ray Allen's age nor his ankles were a concern during the NBA Finals.
STUART CAHILL, BOSTON HERALD

@ LOS ANGELES
JUNE 15, 2008

LAKERS
103

CELTICS
98

Below: Kevin Garnett battles Lakers forward Luke Walton during the fourth quarter. MATT STONE, BOSTON HERALD

Opposite: The Lakers' Kobe Bryant jams home two of his team-high 25 points. STUART CAHILL, BOSTON HERALD

LAKERS PUT 17 ON HOLD

>Mark Murphy, *Boston Herald*
June 16, 2008

In an NBA Finals stocked with blown opportunities on both sides, what's one more?

The Celtics have become master escape artists in this series, again climbing out of a big hole in last night's Game 5. This time, however, erasing a 19-point second-quarter deficit merely was a delicious tease.

Though they threatened throughout, the Celts failed to close the deal in a 103-98 loss to the Lakers. The series now shifts back to Boston for Game 6 tomorrow night.

The Celtics squandered a 38-point performance from a bullish Paul Pierce, who scored 16 from the line and attacked from wire to wire. He gave his team a chance to clinch the franchise's first title in 22 years on the Lakers' hardwood, but instead the Celtics' edge in the series shrunk to 3-2. The only comforting fact is that the final two games are at TD Banknorth Garden.

"Not what we wanted," coach Doc Rivers said. "We wanted two more (wins in LA). Obviously the blanket was that we get to go home, but we really believed that we could win these games.

"We had our chances in all three. We won one of them, and we'll take it, but that's obviously not all that we wanted. . . . We're absolutely disappointed that we couldn't close it out tonight. Guys are down and upset because they thought they could do that, and they thought they should. But we played all year to go home and to have homecourt, and that's what we have now."

Kevin Garnett, forced to play more of an inside role on defense because of the absence of injured Kendrick Perkins, fell into early foul trouble, and that had a

Left: James Posey goes horizontal in the third quarter. MATT STONE, BOSTON HERALD

Opposite: Paul Pierce drives the lane against the Lakers' Vladimir Radmanovic in the second quarter. Pierce scored a game-high 38 points in the loss. MATT STONE, BOSTON HERALD

prolonged effect on the Celtics.

But the Lakers ultimately prevailed thanks to the rarely seen playmaking ability of Kobe Bryant, who took control of the game at both ends.

The league MVP scored seven of his 25 points in the fourth quarter, including five in the final 2:14. But it was his defense, and two steals on Pierce in the last three minutes, that turned the outcome.

"He made a great defensive play," Pierce said of Bryant's ability to fight around a Garnett pick and poke the ball away from the Celtics captain, capping the play with a fast-break dunk that gave the Lakers a 99-95 lead with 37 seconds left. "Kobe's a great player, and he had two big steals on me in the fourth."

Bryant took a relatively modest path.

"I just try to react to the ball," he said. "I want to react to what's in front of me, and to take advantage of that."

It also helped that the Lakers, with Lamar Odom adding 20 points and Pau Gasol chipping in 19, received one of their most balanced performances of the series.

The Celtics made their final threat when Eddie House cut the lead to 101-98 on a 3-pointer with 14.7 seconds left, but Derek Fisher (15 points) had the final say with two free throws.

James Posey landed a haymaker when he buried a trey that cut the Lakers' lead to 90-86 with 5:47 left. Pierce hit his fifth and sixth free throws of the quarter, and the next time down drove and fed Garnett for a 90-90 tie, capping a 16-2 Celts run.

But Gasol posted Garnett for a 92-90 Lakers lead, and after Garnett was only able to hit the second of two free throws at the other end, Odom hit two for a 94-91 edge.

Bryant pulled off his first strip of Pierce, triggering a fast break that resulted in a Fisher free throw and a 95-91 lead. Pierce then drove and was fouled, hitting both with 2:56 left.

A miss by Gasol was forgiven by two Garnett misses from the line. Bryant then hit two free throws, Pierce rebounded his miss at the other end and missed again, and the Celts captain eventually hit two free throws to cut the margin to 97-95 with 1:14 left.

Fisher missed a 20-footer and Pierce went up to pull down a powerful rebound, but Bryant poked the ball away from him again, this time getting the dunk and a four-point cushion.

Ray Allen (16 points) and Garnett (13 points, 14 rebounds) missed — the latter on a tip attempt — and Fisher hit the second of two, setting up a trip back to Boston.

CELTICS
131
LAKERS
92

Below: Paul Pierce, left, and Kevin Garnett celebrate with head coach Doc Rivers as Lakers star Kobe Bryant walks off the floor. MATT STONE, BOSTON HERALD

Opposite: Kevin Garnett drives to the net against the Lakers' Pau Gasol. Garnett finished with 26 points and a game-high 14 rebounds in Boston's clinching victory. MATT STONE, BOSTON HERALD

GLORY GOES TO CELTICS

>Mark Murphy, *Boston Herald*

June 18, 2008

With 4:01 left, Doc Rivers made like Carol Burnett and tugged on his left ear.

As the crowd wailed, "Hey, hey, hey, goodbye," to the Lakers, Glen Davis, Leon Powe and Tony Allen replaced Paul Pierce, Ray Allen and Kevin Garnett.

The Big Three attempted to leave the floor, but the bear hugs that awaited them from Kendrick Perkins, P.J. Brown and Sam Cassell had blocked traffic leading to the bench. Referee Joe Crawford pushed them all off the floor to resume play.

The Celtics were about to win the NBA-record 17th title in franchise history with last night's 131-92 Game 6 victory over the Lakers. The 39-point gap was the largest winning margin in a clinching game in NBA Finals history.

But Rivers remained stoic, his arms crossed.

Danny Ainge, the director of basketball operations who had been on the verge of tears when his picture was put up on the Jumbotron, was now being hugged to death by Garnett in the middle of the huddle.

Rivers, barely a year after pulling into the dock with a 24-win team, stood with his arms crossed to the end. But his calm was finally washed away when Pierce came up from behind and doused him with a bucket of red Gatorade. The coach turned and hugged his captain.

Someone passed him a cell phone and it was Gov. Deval Patrick, offering congratulations instead of the reprieve that would have been the only reason to call last year.

Most of all, Rivers thought about his late father, Grady Rivers, who passed away in November.

Left: Paul Pierce douses head coach Doc Rivers with Gatorade in the waning moments as the Celtics beat the Lakers in Game 6 of the NBA Finals. MATTHEW WEST, BOSTON HERALD

Opposite: Celtics owner Wyc Grousbeck hoists the championship trophy, the 17th in the team's history. MATTHEW WEST, BOSTON HERALD

As was the case in Los Angeles when he was asked the question last week, Rivers teared up last night.

"Well, I thought I was going to get through this," he said, stopping for a moment. "It was the first thing I thought of. I thought of my wife, my kids, my mom. My first thought was what would my dad say, and honestly I started laughing because I thought he would probably say, if you knew my dad, 'It's about time. What have you been waiting for?' So that was my first thought."

His second one undoubtedly had nothing to do with the Lakers, who, after cutting the Celtics' lead in this series to 3-2 with a narrow Game 5 win at Staples Center, barely merited an afterthought last night.

From the rowdy fan in a Kobe Bryant jersey who was escorted out of the arena by security at halftime to the LA star himself, who shot a miserable 7-for-22 for his 22 points, the Garden was no place for a Laker in Game 6.

Not only did the Lakers shoot 42.2 percent, including a 23 percent second quarter when the Celtics broke the game open, they also lost their spirit early. They were outrebounded by a 48-29 margin and turned the ball over 19 times to the Celtics' eight.

The Celtics won almost all of the telltale races for loose balls and rebounds, and before long the lethargy was evident in the Lakers defense as well.

The Celtics blew this one out of reach with a pair of murderous second-quarter runs (11-0, 9-0), hit their first 30-point lead in the third, and coasted home with some wild numbers.

Rajon Rondo, after struggling through three hesitant games in Los Angeles, set the tone by constantly pressuring the ball for six steals in a performance that also included 21 points, eight assists and seven rebounds.

Even with 26 points apiece from Garnett and Allen — the latter tying an NBA Finals record with seven 3-pointers — and a 17-point, 10-assist double-double from Pierce, Rondo was the player turning the corner on the most significant night for a Celtic in 22 years.

MATT STONE, BOSTON HERALD

CELTICS REGULAR SEASON STATISTICS

PLAYER	G	GS	MPG	FG%	3p%	FT%	REBOUNDS OFF	DEF	TOT	APG	SPG	BPG	TO	PPG
Paul Pierce	80	80	35.9	.464	.392	.843	.70	4.50	5.10	4.5	1.26	.45	2.76	19.6
Kevin Garnett	71	71	32.8	.539	.000	.801	1.90	7.30	9.20	3.4	1.41	1.25	1.94	18.8
Ray Allen	73	73	35.9	.445	.398	.907	1.00	2.60	3.70	3.1	.89	.22	1.74	17.4
Rajon Rondo	77	77	29.9	.492	.263	.611	1.00	3.20	4.20	5.1	1.68	.17	1.91	10.6
Leon Powe	56	5	14.4	.572	.000	.710	1.70	2.40	4.10	.3	.27	.29	.77	7.9
Sam Cassell (BOSTON)	17	1	17.6	.385	.409	.840	.30	1.50	1.80	2.1	.53	.18	1.12	7.6
Sam Cassell (TOTAL)	55	34	23.1	.438	.303	.882	.30	2.20	2.50	3.9	.67	.11	1.76	11.2
Eddie House	78	2	19.0	.409	.393	.917	.20	1.90	2.10	1.9	.76	.13	.97	7.5
James Posey	74	2	24.6	.418	.380	.809	.40	3.90	4.40	1.5	.97	.26	.88	7.4
Kendrick Perkins	78	78	24.5	.615	.000	.623	1.90	4.20	6.10	1.1	.40	1.46	1.60	6.9
Tony Allen	75	11	18.3	.434	.316	.762	.50	1.80	2.20	1.5	.83	.28	1.45	6.6
Glen Davis	69	1	13.6	.484	.000	.660	1.40	1.60	3.00	.4	.45	.29	.94	4.5
P.J. Brown	18	0	11.6	.341	.000	.688	1.60	2.20	3.80	.6	.28	.44	.56	2.2
Gabe Pruitt	15	0	6.3	.359	.250	.500	.10	.50	.50	.9	.33	.00	.33	2.1
Scot Pollard	22	0	7.9	.522	.000	.682	.60	1.00	1.70	.1	.14	.27	.23	1.8
Brian Scalabrine	48	9	10.7	.309	.326	.750	.50	1.20	1.60	.8	.19	.17	.54	1.8
Team Averages	82	0	240.9	.475	.381	.771	10.1	31.9	42.0	22.4	8.5	4.6	15.2	100.5
Opponents	82	0	240.9	.419	.316	.743	11.0	27.9	38.9	18.8	7.2	4.7	16.0	90.3

STATISTICS

CELTICS POST SEASON STATISTICS

PLAYER	G	GS	MPG	FG%	3p%	FT%	REBOUNDS OFF	DEF	TOT	APG	SPG	BPG	TO	PPG
Kevin Garnett	26	26	38.0	.495	.250	.810	2.80	7.80	10.50	3.3	1.35	1.12	2.12	20.4
Paul Pierce	26	26	38.1	.441	.361	.802	.80	4.20	5.00	4.6	1.08	.31	3.15	19.7
Ray Allen	26	26	38.0	.428	.396	.913	1.00	2.80	3.80	2.7	.92	.31	1.46	15.6
Rajon Rondo	26	26	32.0	.407	.250	.691	1.50	2.60	4.10	6.6	1.73	.31	1.81	10.2
James Posey	26	0	22.0	.437	.398	.875	.50	3.10	3.60	1.1	1.00	.31	.54	6.7
Kendrick Perkins	25	25	25.2	.585	.000	.678	2.10	4.00	6.10	.5	.60	1.28	1.24	6.6
Leon Powe	23	1	11.7	.493	.000	.667	1.40	1.30	2.70	.2	.00	.13	.52	5.0
Sam Cassell	21	0	12.6	.333	.214	.824	.10	.60	.70	1.2	.38	.05	.57	4.5
P.J. Brown	25	0	13.6	.464	.000	.840	.70	1.60	2.40	.5	.20	.40	.48	2.9
Eddie House	21	0	7.9	.304	.355	.875	.10	1.00	1.00	.9	.24	.05	.19	2.5
Glen Davis	17	0	8.1	.412	.000	.611	.70	.80	1.50	.4	.29	.24	.59	2.3
Tony Allen	15	0	4.3	.563	.000	.400	.10	.10	.20	.2	.13	.00	.07	1.3
Team Averages	26	0	240.0	.447	.359	.783	11.1	28.9	40.0	21.5	7.6	4.3	12.8	94.0
Opponents	26	0	240.0	.426	.329	.762	9.8	26.5	36.3	18.5	6.1	5.0	14.2	88.8

Boston Herald

The entire staff of the Boston Herald photography department contributed to the coverage of the Boston Celtics season, which culminated in the World Championship. We gratefully acknowledge the efforts of staff photographers and freelancers:

Michael Adaskaveg
Stuart Cahill
Tara Carvalho
Ted Fitzgerald
Mark Garfinkel
Lisa Hornak
Nancy Lane
Faith Ninivaggi
Angela Rowlings
Matt Stone
Matthew West
Patrick Whittemore
John Wilcox

and

Jim Mahoney, Director of Photography
Ted Ancher, Assistant Director
Arthur Pollock, Assistant Director

CREDITS